Rebecca
Hardy

OUR LOVING GOD—
A SUN
AND SHIELD

For the Lord God *is* a sun and shield: the Lord will give grace and glory: no good *thing* will he withhold from them that walk uprightly.
O Lord of hosts, blessed *is* the man that trusteth in thee.

—Psalm 84:11-12

THOMAS B. WARREN, Ph.D.

Published by
NATIONAL CHRISTIAN PRESS, INC.
P. O. Box 1001
Jonesboro, Arkansas 72401

OUR LOVING GOD—
A SUN AND SHIELD

Printed by
WILLIAMS PRINTING COMPANY
Nashville, Tenn.

To the Memory of
MY FATHER AND MOTHER
and the
FATHER AND MOTHER
OF MY WIFE
for all I owe to them
and to
ALL WHO IN THIS LIFE SUFFER TRIBULATION
for what I hope God will mean to them in
their suffering and sorrow, I dedicate this little
volume with my love and best wishes.

CONTENTS

Preface 7

    I. "In the World Ye Have Tribulation" 9

   II. Causes and Sources of Suffering 15

  III. Jesus Is the Friend the Sufferer Needs 28

  IV. The Lord Helps the Sufferer to
Properly Evaluate Suffering 37

    V. The Benefits of Suffering 42

  VI. The Dangers of Suffering 62

 VII. How to Prepare for Suffering 67

VIII. How to Endure Suffering with Patience 78

  IX. Some Good Examples of How
Suffering Should Be Endured 94

   X. Some Lessons Learned and
Conclusions Drawn 103

PREFACE

The material which is in this book was gathered over a period of about five years. This gathering began because of a number of reasons. In conversations with people who were suffering, I thought I saw a real need for a small book which would help the sufferer and his loved ones not only to understand his suffering but to grow spiritually because of suffering. The first writing that I did on this subject came during a relatively minor encounter which I myself had with suffering in 1958. Some thoughts which occurred to me at that time were written down and filed away with the intention of some day doing more work in this vital field.

In the Fall of 1962, I received an invitation from Pepperdine College, Los Angeles, California, to speak on the subject "Christ, Our Contemporary in Suffering," during its 1963 Spring Lectureship. I welcomed the opportunity to give further study to this topic which had been on my mind a great deal for several years. In preparing for that lecture, I prepared and delivered a series of seven sermons on the general subject of human suffering. This series of sermons was preached to the Eastridge Church of Christ, Fort Worth, Texas, a congregation with which I have labored as evangelist for more than ten years.

After the series of sermons and the one lecture had

been delivered, I decided to give further study to this subject and to expand the material into a book. I was especially encouraged to do this by a nurse who heard the sermons. She told me that there were many sick people who needed such material. Of course, it is hoped that the contents of this book will be of great interest to everyone, for there is a real sense in which adversity should be regarded as "chronic"—not merely sporadic –throughout life.

I hope that each reader will study carefully and prayerfully all of the references to the Scriptures which are given in the footnotes throughout the book. To some readers, these footnotes may appear to be too extensive, but I have wanted to point the reader not to my own words but to the *Word of God*. It is to *God* that the sufferer must go to find the explanation for his suffering and to gain the comfort which he seeks. The words of no mere man do either of these. In Chapter IX the reader will find many passages of Scripture written out in full. This chapter should be read over and over by those who are suffering. The Word of God which is quoted in that Chapter should give strength, comfort, assurance, and hope to those who suffer.

It is my prayer that this book will help every reader to see that the Lord wants to be the SUN AND SHIELD for each and every one of us.

—THOMAS B. WARREN

CHAPTER I

"IN THE WORLD YE HAVE TRIBULATION"

Jesus said, "In the world ye have tribulation . . ."[1] Almost every day each one of us sees for himself the truthfulness of this statement. Tribulation, adversity, pain, suffering, and misery among human beings can be seen by almost anyone on any given day.

Some people suffer because of illness. Others suffer because of loss of loved ones. Still others suffer because of some accident. Some of this adversity is difficult for people to understand.

A little boy cries out, "I prayed for my Mommy, but God didn't make her well! I do not believe God is good! I do not even believe in God!"

A mother, torn by grief because her little girl has been run over by an automobile and killed, wails from the depths of her misery, "Why did it happen? I just cannot understand why God let such a thing happen. How can God be good and then allow this to happen?"

A husband referring to his wife in a hospital bed, says to a friend, "My wife has been a good woman all

---

1. John 16:33

of her life. She has tried to live the Christian life as
best she could. But now she is suffering untold misery
with this disease she has. Since she has tried so hard
to serve God, why is He letting her suffer this way?
This is a real strain on my faith."

A woman, lying in her hospital bed with pain rack-
ing her wasted body, cries out within herself, "Oh why
has this happened to me? What have I done to deserve
such pain and misery? I may be dying, and I do not
want to leave my family. Why, oh why am I suffering
so? Can God be good if He allows me to die while
my children are still so young?"

A man whose business has been ruined by malicious
slander, sits alone in his office, with his desk piled high
with overdue bills which he cannot pay, saying to himself, "What have I done to deserve this? I tried to conduct all of my business affairs in the way God would
have me to do it. But now these men have ruined me
by slander. How could the Lord have let this happen
to me? Have I been wrong in believing that God is
kind and benevolent?"

A woman whose body has a malignant growth lies
in her hospital bed waiting for the attendants to take
her to the operating room. She is afraid, very much
afraid. She says to herself, "I thought I had faith, but
now I find that I have so very little faith. I cannot seem
to get hold of myself. Why can I not lift up my eyes

to God and pray in real faith for strength and comfort? Something has been wrong in my efforts to live the Christian life. I have not prepared myself for this in the way I should have."

Such statements as the above are often spoken, some outwardly to others, some inwardly in the heart of the sufferer. Unless there is some answer from God, these questions will remain unanswered. But each person can be thankful that we do have answers from God to these questions. Those answers are found in the Bible, God's revelation to man. God intends for that Word to be of great comfort to man in the hours of his affliction. Centuries ago the Psalmist declared, "This is my comfort in my affliction: for thy word hath quickened me."[2]

One in the midst of great suffering or tribulation might well be compared to a person in a cave which is so dark he cannot see and who is being tormented constantly by some pain. In such a situation he needs both *light* (to guide him in the darkness) and some kind of *cover* (to shield him from his pain). The Psalmist gave to man the words of greatest possible comfort when he said,

> For the Lord God is a sun and shield: the Lord will give grace and glory; no good thing will he withhold from them that walk uprightly. O Lord of hosts, blessed is the man that trusteth in thee.[3]

This wonderful passage pictures God as being the very

---

2. Psalms 119:50.
3. Psalms 84:11, 12.

things which man needs: (1) *light,* to dispel the darkness, and (2) a *shield,* to protect against dangers. These two figures have an especially fine application to the problems of suffering. Many people in the midst of suffering are truly in spiritual darkness. They are bewildered by what is happening to them. They can neither understand it nor see the way out of it. They have no shield with which to guard themselves against the pain, the affliction, and the sheer burden of the situation. How much then do such people need a "Sun" and a "Shield"!

In ordinary times, when men think of the sun, they think of the source of light. They think of warmth, good cheer, vitality, strength, beauty, and fruitfulness. Many times the sufferer (especially those who have suffered for a long time) come to dread the night. They dread that time of night when all of the others in the family are asleep, but they, the sufferers, lie awake because of both the pain which tears at their bodies and the fear which torments their spirits. How, in the midst of the long dreary hours of the night, they long for the light of the morning sun! How they long for the first faint rays of light in the eastern sky. How blessed to the sufferer is the light of the sun!

In ancient times, soldiers depended a great deal upon their shields. There were two types of shields. One was very large. It covered and protected the entire body. The other type was small. It was used when more agile fighting was required. Surely our Lord is like the large one, protecting the whole man from the burdens of his life. This God does in the sense of providing him with the strength and wisdom to bear suffering in the right way. God is man's shield by giving him sufficient resources with which to meet the trials and tribulations of life.

Life is a great battlefield which will be fought in darkness and without protection by those who live without God. Those who live without God simply do not have adequate resources with which to meet suffering.

This passage, Psalms 84:11, 12, further explains that God gives grace and glory to those who walk uprightly. Note that this is a promise which involves *grace,* not merit, yet it is a promise which is carefully qualified. Our Lord will withhold no *good* thing from those who walk uprightly. This does not mean that God will necessarily give to the sufferer everything for which he asks. It *does* mean that God will not forsake the righteous sufferer and will give him what is best for him to have. God will withhold "no *good* thing."

Perhaps you, the reader, are, at this very moment, in the midst of great suffering. You or one of your family may be very ill. You may have lost through death your dearly beloved wife, husband, child, mother or father. You may be bewildered by many things you do not understand. You may be tragically afraid of what is now happening to you and what you envision may yet happen. If this is the case, *does* the Bible have a message for your heart? Yes, it does! Oh, how happy the author of this book is to tell you that the Bible *does* have a message for your troubled heart. God is our Refuge and Fortress.[4] He is our Rock and our Salvation.[5] He is our high Tower.[6] He is a Sun and Shield for troubled hearts.[7]

God will help us in our suffering. He knows our weaknesses and our needs. He "knoweth our frame; he remembers that we are dust."[8] Blessed be the name of the Lord.

4. Psalms 91:2.
5. Psalms 62.6.
6. Psalms 18:2.
7. Psalms 84:11, 12.
8. Psalms 103:14.

CHAPTER II

THE CAUSES AND SOURCES
OF SUFERING

Suffering comes in one form or another, either directly or indirectly, to every person. Suffering is not confined to classes. It is found everywhere among all nations and races.

Some people suffer intensely over a long period of time. Others do not suffer quite so much. But every person becomes acquainted, at least to some degree, with disease, bereavement, fear, poverty, anxiety, and many other kinds of tribulations and suffering.

Suffering comes to those who are not Christians. It also comes to those who are Christians. One must not conclude that being a Christian guarantees him freedom from disease and pain. Well did Job say, "Man that is born of woman is of few days, and full of trouble . . . His flesh upon him shall have pain, and his soul within him shall mourn."[1]

QUESTIONS WHICH PEOPLE ASK
ABOUT SUFFERING

As has already been suggested, those who suffer ask

---

1. Job 14:1, 22.

questions which spring from their misery. Here are some of them. Why do men suffer? Do only the wicked suffer? If righteous men suffer, then how can God be both infinitely good and infinitely powerful? What are the causes of suffering? What part, if any, does Satan play in man's suffering? Can Jesus Christ be counted on as a friend during suffering? What is the right way to react to suffering? Are there any people who would continue to serve God in spite of great suffering? Are there any benefits of suffering? Should man learn any lessons from his suffering? How can one best prepare to meet suffering?

A "DILEMMA" POSED BY SOME

After considering the great amount of suffering which mankind endures, some people have concluded that one of two propositions must be true. They say that the presence of evil in the world proves that God is either (1) *good* (and thus wishes man to be free of the suffering) but is too *weak* to do anything about it, or (2) *strong* (and thus has the power to rid man of suffering) but is not benevolent — that is, He simply does not wish to do so. Such people have told others that this is a true dilemma and that all men must choose one or the other of these two propositions. But it is not a true dilemma because it does not exhaust all of the possibilities. This so-called dilemma says nothing of the fact that God by His own choice gave to man freedom of will. When God created man, He gave to him the power of choice. He gave to man the intellectual and spiritual capacity to choose between what is right and what is wrong. He gave man the power to choose between serving God and serving Satan. When man, in exercising that freedom, chose to violate God's instructions (thus becoming guilty of sin), he also had to suffer the consequences of his evil choice.

UNDERSTANDING GOD'S WILL IS THE KEY WHICH UNLOCKS THE SOLUTION

God's will in the ideal sense. When God created man, it was His desire that man would be truly happy. He put man into a situation where he was in possession of everything he needed to make him happy and was free from everything that could make him unhappy — save as he (man), by his own *wrong* choice, would make it so. God gave to man everything he needed from a *physical* standpoint. He lacked for nothing in the Garden of Eden. Of this the Bible says,

> And the Lord God planted a garden eastward in Eden; and there he put the man whom he had formed. And out of the ground made the Lord God to grow every tree that is pleasant to the sight, and good for food; the tree of life also in the midst of the garden, and the tree of knowledge of good and evil. And a river went out of Eden to water the garden . . .[2]

God also gave *woman* to man to be a helper perfectly

---

2. Genesis 2:8-10.

suited to him.[3] Woman was everything man needed
in the way of human companionship. And God also gave
to man fellowship with Himself. God was in direct com-
munication and intimate fellowship with the man whom
He had created. These matters show the will of God
for man in the *ideal* sense. At this stage of his life,
man endured no pain, no sorrow, no disease, no tears,
no death, no anxiety. God loved man and wanted him
to have this kind of situation. Yet in order to have man
to worship Him because of man's love for God (and
thus making his own choice to serve God), God also
had to give man the freedom to not love God. This
means that God had to give to man the freedom to
choose *not* to serve Him. It was not God's will that
man would sin, but, in order for man to be man, God
had to give him freedom of choice — freedom to choose
to serve either God or Satan. Genesis 3 contains the
account of man's fall into sin.

God's will in the circumstance of man's sin. When
man sinned, he deserved eternal separation from God in
a place of punishment.[4] From a standpoint of strict justice, when man sinned God would have cast him off forever. However, because of His love for man, God had a
plan by which man could be saved from his sin. This
plan involved the shedding of the blood of Jesus Christ,
the Son of God.[5] This plan was first intimated when

3. Genesis 2:18.
4. Romans 6:23.
5. Romans 5:8, 9.

God said to the serpent (after man's fall), "And I will
put enmity between thee and the woman, and between
thy seed and her seed; it shall bruise thy head, and thou
shalt bruise his heel."[6] The "seed of the woman" (reference is to the Virgin Birth of Christ) was to be the
one by whom man could be saved from his sins. God
spent the long years of the Old Testament (from the
days of Adam to the days of Christ) in bringing the world
situation to just what was needed ("the fulness of the
time"[7]) for the coming of Christ. After having lived a
perfect life, the Lord Jesus Christ was crucified, shedding
His blood that man might be saved.[8] After He was raised
from the dead, He gave to His Apostles the commission
to go into all the world and preach the Gospel to every
creature. Those who comply with the terms of that
Gospel shall be saved by the blood of Christ.[9] God's
love for man is manifested in the gift of His Son and
in the Gospel plan of salvation.[10]

God's will for eternity. This might be referred to as
God's ultimate will. It is God's ultimate will to bless all
of the righteous by giving them an eternal home in·
heaven and to punish all of the wicked by casting them
into hell.[11] There is no single power, there is no com·

---

6. Genesis 3:15.
7. Galatians 4:4.
8. Ephesians 1:7.
9. Mark 16:15, 16.
10. John 3:16.
11. Matthew 25:46.

bination of powers which can prevent God's accomplish-
ment of this ultimate will. Men may reject God's will
to believe on Jesus Christ as the Son of God; they may
refuse to obey the terms set forth in the Gospel. But
some day all men will stand before God in Judgment
to give an account for the deeds done in the body.[12]

The preceeding facts show, among other things, the
following: (1) that it is the ideal or intentional will of
God for man to be happy and free from sorrow and
pain; (2) that God loves man so much and wishes so
much for man to be blessed that He gave His Son to die
for man; (3) that each man who sins and refuses to
repent of his sin thereby cuts himself off from the blessings which God wishes to give him; (4) the pain, sorrow, suffering, tears, and death *which is in the world is
here* because of man's sins; (5) God is infinitely powerful, and infinitely wise. The fact that there is suffering
in the world means neither that God is weak nor that
God is not benevolent. It means that God has given man
freedom to make choices and that man has made and
continues to make many evil choices.

SOME CAUSES OF SUFFERING
AMONG MANKIND

The entire field of suffering is a very complex one.
In one sense, it can be truthfully said that all suffering
is the result of sin. But it is of value to the sufferer to

12. II Corinthians 5:1-11.

look at the matter in a little more detail. Many of the readers of this book, from the depths of their hearts may be asking, "Why am I suffering? What is the meaning or the significance of it? What has caused it? Have *I* done something wrong? Is God *punishing* me for some *sin* in my life?" To understand the various sources or causes of suffering will be helpful in answering such questions.

Some suffering comes as a result of ignorance. Simply because they do not understand the basic rules of health, some people drink impure water or eat contaminated food. Then they become ill and suffer. Sometimes they die as a result of such action. In 1962 many women took a drug which caused them to give birth to extremely mal-formed babies. Both the parents and the babies are suffering as a result of the mothers having taken a drug, the effects of which they were ignorant.

Some suffering comes as a result of accidents. Many people fall in their own homes and injure themselves. At times such injuries cause great suffering. Others have suffered because of injuries sustained in an automobile accident. Some people may be in either a bed or a wheelchair for a long time as the result of such accidents. Not long ago one of the finest athletes in the world fell and broke his neck. He now is paralyzed from the neck down.

Some suffering comes as a result of living in a world

into which sin has come. As has already been explained, before man sinned, there was no human suffering in the world.[13] This fact is helpful in understanding God's benevolent attiude toward man. But the consequences of sin entering the world have been and continue to be terrible and far-reaching. Because men live in a world which has been afflicted by sin, they sometimes are stricken with such dreaded diseases as cancer. As a result they suffer a great deal. Their families also suffer with them. Each person faces both death and the possibility of seeing a loved one taken from him by death. Each person faces the heart-breaking procession to the cemetery to leave the body of one who is more dear than life itself. Death entered the world through sin.

Some people suffer because of the sins of others. At times people suffer from the sins of other people, not from their own sins. Some people who are God-fearing and law abiding have been mangled or killed on the highway as the result of the reckless driving of a drunken driver who is disobeying both the law of God and the law of man. Innocent little children at times suffer extreme anguish, poverty, and even beatings by a drunken father. Babies are sometimes born blind because of the sins of the parents. Godly men are persecuted in numerous ways by evil men. In the days of the New Testament, some faithful Christians were thrown into arenas to be devoured by famished beasts for the purpose of

---

13. Genesis 2.

entertaining evil men. Because some evil men have lusted for great power, other millions have spent their lives under horrible oppression.

Some people suffer as a result of their own sins. After starting out well, King Saul of Israel became an ungodly man. He suffered in many ways because of his own sins.[14] Jacob, a grandson of Abraham, was another man who suffered because of his own sins.[15] Likely each reader of this book has knowledge of men who had wonderful wives and children but who became drunkards and lost them. Many homes have been destroyed, and much suffering has resulted from husbands or wives being unfaithful to the sacred vows of marriage. The bodies of many people are now racked with pain and ravaged with decay because of sensual debauchery. Close ties of friendship have been broken because of sin. Because of the sin of worry and anxiety, many suffer anguish day by day. Worry and anxiety basically come as a result of a lack of faith. It is sin to lack faith (Hebrews 11:6; Philippians 4:6, 7).

Some suffering comes as the result of God's providence working in the affairs of men. Joseph, the favorite son of Jacob, suffered a great deal because the Lord's providence worked in such fashion as to bring him into Egypt at the right time under the right circumstances to

---

14. I Samuel 9-31.
15. Genesis 25-50.

suit God's purposes.[16] Joseph himself understood that
his brothers, who had sold him into slavery, had meant
for harm to come to him but that God had meant it for
good.[17] The entire nation of Israel suffered as a result
of God's providence in the matter of bringing Jacob and
his family down into Egypt from Canaan. This nation
being put under bondage and later freed from that bondage in passing through the Red Sea is a wonderful illus-
tration to help men today understand the Gospel plan of
salvation.[18] God's providence may be at work at this very
moment in the life of the reader of this book.

*Some suffering comes to people because they try to
walk in the footsteps of Christ.* Jesus warned His disciples,
"In the world ye have tribulation . . ."[19]

Paul exhorted, "Suffer hardship with me, as a good
soldier of Christ Jesus."[20] Peter urged, "Beloved, think
it not strange concerning the fiery trial among you to
prove you . . ."[21] Paul also warned, "Yea, and all that
live godly in Christ Jesus shall suffer persecution."[22]

*Some suffering comes as a result of man's being
chastened by the Lord.* The writer of Hebrews said,
". . . whom the Lord loveth he chasteneth, and scourgeth

16. Genesis 30-50.
17. Genesis 50:20.
18. Exodus 14:30; I Corinthians 10:1-4.
19. John 16:33.
20. II Timothy 2:3.
21. I Peter 4:12.
22. II Timothy 3:12.

every son whom he receiveth."[23] The Lord chastened Paul with a "thorn in the flesh."[24] This "thorn" was given to him so that he would "not be exalted overmuch."[25] The Lord chastens man that man might be benefitted. When one properly reacts to suffering, he will repent of his sins and turn to God. The Psalmist said, "Before I was afflicted I went astray: but now I have kept thy word."[26]

Some suffering comes as a result of testing to which men are subjected. God commanded Abraham to offer his son Isaac as a sacrifice. Abraham obeyed God without wavering through unbelief.[27] Any father who truly loves his son could well understand the anguish which Abraham endured as he thought of sacrificing his son, even though he believed that God would raise that son from the dead. Even though Job was a righteous man, God allowed Satan to test him by causing him to endure almost indescribable suffering.[28] In much the same way, Peter and the other Apostles were tested by Satan.[29]

Some suffering comes as a result of man's having to go from this life to the next. Every man faces death,[30] and death has its sting.[31] Most people face death with

---

23. Hebrews 12:6.
24. II Corinthians 12:7-10.
25. *Ibid.*
26. Psalms 119:67.
27. Hebrews 11:17-19.
28. Book of Job.
29. Luke 22:31, 32.
30. Hebrews 9:27.
31. I Corinthians 15:15.

dread and misgivings. Few people can contemplate without sorrow the thought of leaving family, friends, and neighbors. Most people have a few more things they wish to do before they go. They wish to be a while longer on earth with those they love. Even the act of dying often involves suffering.

Some people will suffer because they refused God's gracious offer of salvation through His Son — Jesus Christ. When Christ comes again, all who are in the graves shall hear His voice and come forth. Those who have lived in harmony with *God's will* will go away into everlasting life. Those who have not lived in harmony with *God's will* will go away into everlasting punishment.[32] It is not the ideal will of God that any person should suffer this fate[33] but some reject God's love and refuse to obey Him. As a result, they must suffer throughout the unending ages of eternity.[34]

HOW CAN ONE KNOW THE CAUSE OR SOURCE OF HIS OWN SUFFERING?

One cannot *always* know the cause of his own particular suffering. In some cases he *can* know; in other cases he cannot know for certain. If one has fallen from a ladder and has broken his back in so doing, he will know the reason why his legs are paralyzed. If one has

32. John 5:28, 29; Matthew 25:46; Revelation 20:10-15.
33. II Peter 3:9.
34. II Thessalonians 1:7-9.

eaten contaminated food, he may well know the reason why he suffers such agony in his stomach. If he has committed a social sin and has contaminated himself with a loathsome disease, he will know the reason for his suffering. There are other situations in which one could know for certain the cause of his suffering. But such cannot be known for certain in every case of suffering. Among other things, this unknown quality makes suffering such a great test of one's faith in and love for the Lord. A more detailed explanation of this matter will be set forth when the story of the suffering of Job is considered in the book.

CHAPTER III

JESUS IS THE FRIEND THE SUFFERER NEEDS

We all need true friends. Even when things are going well, every person needs at least one true friend. Even when a person is not suffering, he needs a true friend. Why is this true? For one thing, men need friends to plead their case when they are slandered. Men need friends to rebuke them when they do wrong. This helps them to get back on the right track. Men need friends to rejoice with them when things go well. Men need friends to weep with them when they are in sorrow. At times, friends are needed to praise some good work which has been done or to praise some valiant stand for truth and righteousness which has been made. Only the truly great can go on without at least a little praise.

Friends offer rest and food in the midst of weariness and hunger. For those who live it well, life involves a lot of hard work. Both minds and bodies become weary at times. Then a friend is needed to offer rest. No one wants to be completely forgotten. Each person wants at least one friend who will not forget him — no matter what happens. In the midst of so much deceit and hypocrisy, each person needs at least one friend who is sincere and faithful, who "sticks by" through "thick and thin." In a complex society where, at times, it is difficult to understand even oneself, each person needs a friend who will at least *try* to understand what one feels and thinks. In a world where there are so many failures and apparent grounds for despondency, each person needs a friend who will reach down a hand by which to give a lift from the depths of despair. For man, Jesus is all of these things and more.

Jesus is the friend the sufferer needs. What a friend we have in Jesus, all our sins and griefs to bear! Jesus truly is the friend the sufferer needs.

Jesus is the friend the sufferer needs because He truly understands what the sufferer is enduring. Often when a person who is enjoying good health visits a person who is very ill, the well person urges the ill one in this fashion, "Buck up; you're going to be all right." No doubt good intentions motivate such an effort, but the sufferer is not helped because he knows the other person does not really understand the suffering. But with Jesus, it is different. He knows all about the suffering. He is able to see the entire situation in which the sufferer is involved as it looks to the sufferer himself. The Lord knows the heart of the sufferer; He knows every thought he has. The Lord Jesus knows what it is to suffer. He knows what it is to be without a friend, for all of His disciples forsook Him as He stood in the very shadow of the cross. He knows what it is to be misunderstood. At first, even His closest disciples did not understand His mission into the world. His enemies misrepresented him over and over again. He knows what it is to be hungry. He knows what it is to be tempted. He knows what it is to be perplexed, and to be in sorrow. He knows what it is to have one's own family to reject Him. He knows what it is to suffer mental anguish. He knows what it is to suffer physically. He endured the horrible suffering of crucifixion. This is why when the sufferer is driven to his knees by his suffering the Lord Jesus truly understands the anguished plea which comes from his lips. When the sufferer cannot even put into words the anguish he feels but can only cry, "Oh, Lord, help me," he may be sure that the Lord hears and understands. He knows what is in man and has no need that anyone should explain it to Him.

Jesus not only understands the sufferer, but He also wants to help. The sufferer may cry out, "Does any one care?" The correct answer is, "Yes, some one does." Jesus cares. He cares when man is lost in sin. He cares when man is in sorrow through the loss of a loved one. He cares when man is suffering. Jesus is the Christian's High Priest. He is not a High Priest who cannot be touched with the feeling of the sufferer's infirmities, but He has also been tempted and understands. He who was rich became poor (came to earth and was crucified) that proverty-stricken man might become rich (in salvation from sin.)[1] On one occasion Jesus looked upon the city of Jerusalem and said, "O Jerusalem, Jerusalem . . . how often would I have gathered thy children together, even as a hen gathereth her chickens under her wings, and ye would not."[2] On another occasion, He said, "Come unto me, all ye that labor and are heavy laden, and I will give you rest."[3]

Jesus will help those in need. God's word plainly teaches that Jesus understands the problem of those who suffer, that He cares, that He wants to help those who need him, and that He will help if men will only allow Him to do so. James said, ". . . ye have not, because ye ask not."[4] At times men do not have blessings from the Lord simply because they do not ask for them. They are much like the old colored man named Sam who (in a story) had served faithfully and well as a slave. His master died and gave the old man both his freedom and a great sum of money. The money was deposited in the man's name in the local bank. Since the old man was now both free and rich, the people of the town expected him to build a fine mansion and live as wealthy men usually live. But he continued to live in a shack and ate only enough food to barely keep him alive. One day a man asked him, "Sam, why don't you go down to the bank, write a check, and get some money so you can

---

1. II Corinthians 8:9.
2. Matthew 23:37.
3. Matthew 11:28.
4. James 4:2.

live comfortably? The money is there for you. Why don't you use it?"

Sam, not really understanding previously that he could obtain the money by just writing a check, hurried down to the bank and wrote a check for *one dollar!* The banker knowing Sam's proverty-stricken way of living said, "Is this all you want, Sam? You know that you can have a lot more if you want it, don't you? All you have to do is write a check."

"No, all I want is enough to buy a sack of flour. I reckon I don't need anything else."

Some Christians, with the untold wealth of God's blessings in the "bank of heaven" do as the old freed slave did. Some do not even ask, so they do not receive. Others ask, but they ask for *trifling* things as the old colored man did in asking only for a sack of flour.

Jesus urged His children to ask for blessings in the full assurance that they would receive what is good for them. "No good things does the Lord withhold."[5]

In the Sermon on the Mount, Jesus said,

Ask, and it shall be given you; seek, and ye shall find; knock, and it shall be opened unto you: For every one that asketh receiveth; and he that seeketh findeth and to him that knocketh it shall be opened. Or what man is there of you, whom if his son ask bread, will he give him a stone? Or if he ask a fish, will he give him a serpent? If ye then, being evil, know how to

5. Psalms 84:11.

give good gifts unto your children, how much more shall
your Father which is in heaven give good things to them
that ask him?[6]

The Lord thus leads men to reason in this fashion:
(1) the Lord is infinitely greater and His love is infinitely
more pure than that of human fathers; (2) human fathers
(who are at least somewhat evil and selfish) give good
things to their own children: (3) thus, men may be sure
that their Heavenly Father will give to them the good
things they need; (4) provided they ask for those blessings in the right way.

In much the same line of thought, the Apostle Paul
said,

What shall we then say to these things? If God be
for us, who can be against us? He that spared not
his own Son, but delivered him up for us all, how shall
he not with him also freely give us all things?[7]

In this passage, Paul makes the following argument
(some of it implied): (1) it is reasonable to conclude
that if God did not fail to spare His own Son for the
good of man, He would not spare anything else for the
good of man; (2) God did not spare His own Son but
delivered Him up for us all; (3) man may rightly conclude that God will give man the good things he needs.

How glorious a passage for any and every man. How
comforting a passage to the sufferer! You are suffer-

---

6. Matthew 7:7-11.
7. Romans 8:31, 32.

ıng? You have need? Live in harmony with His will, then *ask, seek,* and *knock,* and God will not withhold what is good for you from you.

The Psalmist said,

> Yea, though I walk through the valley of the shadow of death, I will fear no evil: for thou art with me; thy rod and thy staff they comfort me. Thou preparest a table before me in the presence of mine enemies: thou anointest my head with oil; my cup runneth over. Surely goodness and mercy shall follow me all the days of my life: and I will dwell in the house of the Lord for ever.[8]

Even while walking through the valley of the shadow of death, the faithful child of God may say, "I will fear no evil . . . Why? . . . for *thou* (the *Lord*) art with me . . ."

Jesus will give to His faithful children peace of mind even in the midst of the most adverse circumstances. The Apostle Paul said,

> Be careful for nothing; but in every thing by prayer and supplication with thanksgiving let your requests be made known unto God. And the peace of God, And the peace of God, which passeth all understanding, shall keep your hearts and minds through Christ Jesus.[9]

Perhaps some burdened sufferer is ready to say, "That *sounds* good, but I prayed and nothing happened." No mere human being has the wisdom to make such a

---

8. Psalms 23:4-6.
9. Philippians 4:6, 7.

statement. It may be true that the thing for which the sufferer asked was not given, but if the sufferer is a faithful child of God then *something* happened when he prayed. The Apostle Peter said,

> For he that will love life, and see good days, let him refrain his tongue from evil, and his lips that they speak no guile: Let him eschew evil, and do good; let him seek peace, and ensue it. For the eyes of the Lord are over the righteous, and his ears are open unto their prayers: but the face of the Lord is against them that do evil.[10]

God will not turn a deaf ear to the pleas of righteous men and women. At times, His answer to prayer may be, *"No,* that is not what is best for you." Or, it may be, "Yes, I will give you that, but it is not best that you have it *now."* Or, the Lord's answer to prayer may be, "I will answer your prayer, but you have not asked for the right thing; I will give you *something else.* I will give you what you need, what is best for you."

God's children must trust Him to do what is best even when they neither see nor understand what is being done. Job said, "Though he slay me, yet will I trust him."[11]

Trust Him, dear burdened sufferer. He will never leave you nor forsake you.

---

10. I Peter 3:10-11.
11. Job 13:15,

LOOK UP!

Look up, dear child—
    The Father watches still,
Keep anchored fast in Him;
    He ever will.

He spoke, a voice so tender,
    Calm and sweet,
The raging billows humbled,
    At His feet.

Don't watch the waves,
    They might cause you to fear,
And you'd forget,
    The Master is so near.

—IRENE MANNEY
(Used by Permission)

CHAPTER IV

THE LORD, THROUGH THE BIBLE, HELPS THE SUFFERER TO PROPERLY EVALUATE HIS SUFFERING

Paul, one of the Lord's Apostles, said,

> For which cause we faint not; but though our outward man perish, yet the inward man is renewed day by day. For our light affliction, which is but for a moment, worketh for us a far more exceeding and eternal weight of glory; While we look not at the things which are seen, but at the things which are not seen: for the things which are seen are temporal; but the things which are not seen are eternal.[1]

In this marvelous passage, Paul described the suffering of God's faithful children as being: (1) light; (2) for the moment; (3) that which makes some contribution to the sufferer's gaining of eternal glory.

It is true, of course, that from a human standpoint of evaluating matters, much suffering is anything but "light"; it is "heavy" indeed. Some people endure suffering which is both very intense and long-lasting. The sufferings of Paul himself were "heavy" by mere human standards. It is evident from these facts and from the text itself that Paul means that human suffering is "light" in a *comparative* sense.

---

1. II Corinthians 4:16-18.

Human suffering is light in comparison with the great goals of a Christian. The basic goals of a Christian are: (1) to so "walk in the light"[2] of God's word that he will be eternally saved; (2) to glorify God by his life[3] — even in suffering; (3) to preach or teach the Gospel in such fashion as to lead others to glorify God and be saved.[4] In comparison with these goals, the suffering of a Christian is both "light" (that is, not very heavy to bear) and "for the moment" (that is, only a brief moment in comparison with the unending ages of eternity).

Human suffering is light in comparison with what the sufferer actually deserves. Paul said, "The wages of sin is death."[5] That death is described by John in the Book of Revelation.[6] It is horrible indeed; it is what every sinner justly deserves, for sin separates the sinner from God[7] and deserves punishment.[8] No suffering in this life can be compared with the suffering of those who are lost in Hell.[9] It is only because of and through God's love for and mercy to man that any sinner could escape the punishment every sinner justly deserves.[10]

Human suffering is light in comparison with the suffering which Jesus endured. Jesus suffered the agony of

---

2. I John 1:7.
3. Matthew 5:16.
4. Philippians 2:14-16.
5. Romans 6:23.
6. Revelation 20:10-15.
7. Isaiah 59:1, 2.
8. See also Mark 9:47, 48; Thessalonians 1:7-9.
9. Revelation 20:10-11.
10. See Ephesians 2:8, 9; John 3:16; Titus 2:11; Romans 5:8, 9.

Gethsemane and endured alone the torture of the cross. To fully comprehend the extent and intensity of the suffering which crucifixion brought upon the one crucified, one would have to spend much time in the study of the entire procedure and the reactions which occur in the human body. One would also have to study the spiritual implications for Jesus.

Human suffering is light in comparison with the blessings of having one's sins forgiven. Suffering can cause the sufferer to turn from sin to serve God. The Psalmist said, "Before I was afflicted, I went astray . . ."[11] In comparison with having one's sins forgiven, it is a small thing to suffer — even from the worst disease — in this life.

Human suffering is light in comparison with having Christ's love to sustain us in times of tribulation. Paul said, ". . . we glory in tribulations also; knowing that tribulation worketh patience."[12] The Psalmist said, "The Lord also will be a refuge for the oppressed in times of trouble."[13] The Psalmist also said, "For in time of trouble he shall hide me in his pavilion: in the secret of his tabernacle shall he hide me; he shall set me upon a rock."[14] Here is another marvelous assurance, "The eternal God is thy refuge, and underneath are the everlasting

---

11. Psalms 119:67.
12. Romans 5:3.
13. Psalms 9:9.
14. Psalms 27:5.

arms . . ."[15] When the sufferer understands and truly
believes in and lays hold on God's love for him, then
his suffering becomes light, even though by ordinary
human standards it is tremendously heavy.

*Human suffering is light in comparison with having
Christ with us in the moment of death.* Christians sing
the old song, "I Won't Have to Cross Jordan Alone."
This means that Christ will be with His faithful child
in the moment of his death. The Psalmist said, "Yea,
though I walk through the valley of the shadow of death,
I will fear no evil: for thou art with me."[16] Loved ones
and friends can stand by the bedside and hold the hand
of the dying, but they can go with the dying only so far.
They cannot cross "Jordan" (the "river" of death) with
them. But Christ will be with His faithful child even in
the valley of the shadow of death. "Precious in the sight
of the Lord is the death of his saints."[17] Surely, any suffering which must be borne is "light" in comparison with
this blessing.

*Human suffering is light in comparison with the glories
of eternity in heaven.* When the faithful Christian dies,
he lifts up his eyes in a place of pleasure. This occurs
even before the Judgment.[18] After the Judgment, God's
faithful children will be given a home in the "land that
is fairer than day," where there will be no pain, no sorrow,

15. Deuteronomy 33:27.
16. Psalms 23:4.
17. Psalms 116:15.
18. Luke 16:19-25.

no tears, no death, and no decay. There will be no night, but one eternal day. There will be no funeral processions, no long hours of vigilance with the sick and dying. But there will be the River of Life and the Tree of Life.[19] What are the sufferings of this world in comparison with the wonders and glories of heaven? Whatever children of God may suffer in this life is truly "light" in comparison with glories and blessings of heaven.

Human suffering is light in comparison with the unending ages of eternity. At times human suffering which goes on for years seems to be of an unbearable length. But suffering of a few years on this earth is "light" in comparison with the unending suffering which shall be the fate of those who die in sin.[20] The length of suffering during life on earth is" light" in comparison with the unending ages of joy which shall come to those who go to heaven.

---

19. Revelation 22:1-3.
20. Matthew 25:46,

CHAPTER V

THE BENEFITS OF SUFFERING

Suffering may be either beneficial or destructive to the sufferer. The result of suffering depends upon the reaction which the suffer makes to it. Suffering may drive one away from faith into despair and utter discouragement — and so, away from God. On the other hand, suffering may lead one to do such soul-searching as will result in repentance from sin, which, in turn, will lead one closer to God. Reacting to suffering is much like reacting to a hot poker: it will burn us or help us, depending upon whether we grasp it by the handle or the hot end. Suffering can terribly scar one if he does not react to it as God would have him to react. But it can be the source of manifold blessing if one does properly react.

Of suffering, Peter said,

> Wherein ye greatly rejoice, though now for a season, if need bē, ye are in heaviness through manifold temptations: That the trial of your faith, being much more precious than of gold that perisheth, though it be tried with fire, might be found unto praise and honour and glory at the appearing of Jesus Christ: Whom having not seen, ye love; in whom, though now ye see him not, yet believing, ye rejoice with joy unspeakable and full of glory: Receiving the end of your faith, even the salvation of your souls.[1]

---

1. I Peter 1:6-9.

Further, Peter said,

> Beloved, think it not strange concerning the fiery trial
> which is to try you, as though some strange thing hap-
> pened unto you: But rejoice, inasmuch as ye are par-
> takers of Christ's sufferings; that, when his glory shall
> be revealed, ye may be glad also with exceeding joy.[2]

Following are some of the benefits which may come
to the sufferer (and perhaps to those who observe his
suffering) *provided* he reacts to the suffering as God
would have him to react.

Suffering helps the sufferer to know himself. One of
the most vital needs of man is to know himself. The
Psalmist prayed in these words,

> Search me, O God, and know my heart: try me, and
> know my thoughts: And see if there be any wicked
> way in me, and lead me in the way everlasting.[3]

When a person faces no great affliction, or suffering,
it is easy for him to give little thought to his true spiritual
condition, as viewed by God. But when the rigors and
trials of adversity and suffering turn one in upon himself
to face squarely what is the true condition of his heart
and life, the person suffering often must face the fact
that he is lacking in faith, in love, and in dedication of
life.

Before he actually was involved in the severe test
(which he failed), Peter viewed himself as a tower of

---

2. I Peter 4:12, 13.
3. Psalms 139:23, 24.

strength.[4] But the actual testing introduced Peter to himself. He found that rather than being strong he was weak. Thus he failed his spiritual test: he denied the Lord.[5] So long as one has a measure of wealth, good health, loving family, good friends, and good reputation, in *appearance* he may have great faith in and love for the Lord. But being plunged into the depths and horror of extreme suffering may cause him to see himself as sadly lacking in both faith and love. It is true that the good and honest heart may learn valuable lessons from times of health and prosperity. It is likely, however, that deeper and more profound lessons are learned from adversity. The long road of sorrow and suffering is a schoolroom in which lessons are learned that can be learned nowhere else. This is why God's children are taught to rejoice in suffering.

Men sometimes pray, as the Psalmist did,[6] for divine aid in knowing themselves. It may be that God answered their prayers by allowing them to be put into the crucible of suffering. This *may* be the case of the reader of this book.

Suffering helps the sufferer to attain a proper set of values. It is easier for a man in the midst of great suffering to see what is really important and what is not important. A man with good health may say to himself,

---

4. Matthew 26:31-35.
5. Matthew 26:69-74.
6. Psalms 139:23, 24.

"Wealth, popularity, position, and pleasure are the most important things in life. I *must* have these things. I will work long hours in order to have them." But to the man who realizes he may be dying, wealth, popularity, and such like have little appeal. The issues of life usually look quite different to the man whose body is wasting away under the ravages of disease from how it looks to the man with good health. To the mother and father whose children are all well, a new car may seem to be the most important thing in life. But to the mother and father whose little boy or girl is at death's door (because of disease or accident), cars, stocks, bonds, bank accounts, popularity, and such comparatively trivial matters are of little or no consequence. One man may be in despair because he has so little money. Another man (who has lost his health) may be fervently wishing that he had no problem but that of money.

When a minister goes to the home of those who have lost loved ones in death, he hears little or no talk of how rich the departed person was. Rather, he hears the family tell of whatever good they can remember about the loved one who has departed. Matters which may seem to be gigantic in importance when one has his health, often fade into the status of being insignificant when one suffers severe affliction or adversity. To the severe sufferer, the question of supreme importance usually is, "Is my life right with God and with my fellowman?"

Suffering helps the sufferer to be thankful for his blessings. The average person takes for granted the blessings which he receives from day to day. He gives little thought to the blessings of his own life; his faithful and loving wife; his children; his brethren in Christ; the various physical blessings of life (food, clothing, shelter, water, air), the privilege of living in a land which provides civil freedom where men have the right to life, liberty, and the pursuit of happiness; the blessing of hearing the Gospel of Christ and the promise of salvation which it offers;[7] the privilege of prayer through Christ; the privilege of the study and practice of the Bible; the privilege of worship.

It is a valuable exercise for any person to prayerfully consider the blessings which he possesses at any given moment and then seek to envision the situation which would follow if he suddenly lost all of these blessings. He would then be faced with the situation in which his wife, his children, his wealth, his home, his friends, his reputation, his health, and other blessings were all taken away. He would be reduced to being a man who was gravely ill, poverty-stricken with neither house, crumb of food, nor coat, benefit of wife, children, friends, and reputation. Each person should carefully contemplate such a situation and then seek to envision what joy would fill his heart if all of these blessings were suddenly given

7. John 3:16; Mark 16:15, 16; Acts 2:36-38; Ephesians 2:8, 9.

back to him. How much more highly he would prize them!

Thus, suffering helps one to see the value of the blessings which men tend to take for granted day by day.

Properly reacted to, suffering helps the sufferer to avoid self-pity. This may seem to be paradoxical, but even from those in the midst of severe suffering it is usually not very far to others whose suffering is even more severe. Proper reaction to suffering leads one to spend time in praying for others. Praying for the welfare of others serves as a guard against pitying oneself.

Suffering helps the sufferer to see the value of prayer. When one is enjoying good health and is prospering financially, it is easy to drift away from a feeling of dependence on God. It is hard for a rich man to sincerely sing that good old song, "I Need Thee Every Hour." But adversity helps the sufferer to see the value of prayer. Adversity helps the sufferer to pray more intensely. Before his severe adversity, Manasseh, king of Judah, was very wicked,[8] but his severe distress caused him to humble himself and to pray to God.[9]

It is extremely difficult, indeed if not impossible, for a sufferer to hold ill-will toward those who deeply, sincerely, and lovingly pray for his welfare. How wonderful

8. II Chronicles 33:9. 10.
9. II Chronicles 33:11-13,

it is to learn of this power to win the love of others. The author of this book has seen love fill his own heart for those who prayed for him. He concludes that it will do the same for others. How great a "balm in Gilead" is prayer for those who suffer. Prayer brings blessings to those who ask as God would have them to ask.[10] God will not turn a deaf ear but will give what is good to those who ask in faith.[11] Thus suffering helps the sufferer to better understand the place which prayer occupies in God's scheme of things. It helps the sufferer to realize that he must keep on praying and not to faint.

Suffering helps the sufferer to understand what a blessing it is not to be able to see what the future holds. Some burdens of life would seem to be more than one could bear if men had full knowledge of the future. But each person is given the load of life one day at a time, and each one must learn to carry only the load of each day as it comes, trusting in the Lord not to allow us to have thrust upon us more than we can bear.[12] Severe suffering tends to lead the sufferer to seek more earnestly the deeper meanings of such passages as Matthew 6:34; Philippians 4:6, 7; and I Peter 5:7. Suffering helps the sufferer to acknowledge God in all his ways and to trust Him to direct him in the best pathways of life.[13]

---

10. Matthew 7:7-11.
11. I Peter 3:10-12.
12. I Corinthians 10:13.
13. Proverbs 3:3-5.

Suffering helps the sufferer to better understand the fatherhood of God. The relationship of God to the saved is that of Father and children. Jesus Himself emphasized this relationship.[14] He taught that if earthly fathers (who are subject to lust, greed, selfishness, and even malice) know how to respond with beneficence to the requests of their own children, how much more should the children of the Heavenly Father expect Him to respond to their proper requests. Suffering makes the understanding of this sublime truth an urgent matter. Because of his suffering, the person who suffers becomes more keenly aware of the need for such understanding. The awareness causes his *search* for such understanding to become more sincere, more intense, and more free from selfish motives and frivolous goals. How vital it is for God's children to be deeply aware of the fatherhood of God! The sufferer who truly is a faithful child of God, and who has great confidence in God as a loving father, has in this confidence as unseen power with which to bear his burden. Jesus taught His disciples to pray, "Our Father, who art in heaven . . ."[15] Intense suffering helps the sufferer to address God as "Father" with deeper meaning and greater significance.

Sufferings helps the sufferer to see better the weakness of himself and the strength of God. When one is in the midst of prosperity and good health, it is easy for

---

14. Matthew 7:7-11.
15. Matthew 6:9.

him to conceive of himself as being strong and needing nothing. But severe suffering strips the self-satisfied of their pride. After Peter had denied the Lord Jesus and had heard the cock crow, he went out and wept — *bitterly*.[16] In contrast to the pride which he had at one time in his own strength, Peter's first epistle is characterized by humility and a recognition of the need for the Lord's strength with which to meet the trials of life.

Suffering helps the sufferer to better understand his own love for others. Most people love their wives (or husbands), children, friends, and brethren in Christ. But acute adversity, and especially such suffering as leads the sufferer to face the possibility that he may have to leave those loved ones through death, helps the sufferer to understand his love for them better than he would have been able to understand it otherwise. Suffering helps the sufferer to see how very much he values his own love for others and their love for him.

Suffering helps the sufferer to overlook the faults and see the good in those whom he loves. Those whom the sufferer loves are only human and thus have faults, weaknesses, and shortcomings — just as the sufferer does. Suffering helps a person to see this fact better than it could be seen otherwise. Because of this, the one who suffers comes to minimize those shortcomings and to emphasize and dwell upon the good in their hearts and

---

16. Matthew 26:75.

lives. A soldier who is thousands of miles away from his wife finds it easy to remember the *good* things about his wife. He finds himself discounting whatever short comings she may have. Adversity helps one to *love* better because it helps one to *see* better.

Sufferings helps one to see the value of the right kind of sympathy. Not all sympathy is good for the one who is suffering. Sympathy which causes the sufferer to be filled with self-pity tends to be destructive. The right kind of sympathy lovingly recognizes the problem and faithfully points the way to the solution. Jesus pointed sufferers to a solution to their suffering. He viewed the suffering through the eyes of the one who was suffering and then pointed the way to the right attitude toward and the right action in the midst of suffering. This should be the aim of all who seek to sympathize with those who are suffering.

By observing efforts which give the wrong kind of sympathy, the sufferer learns better how he himself should sympathize with others.

Suffering helps one to better realize the value of a kind word. When thinking about one who is suffering, the average person is apt to say, "Why bother with saying a kind word to him? It will mean nothing to him." But when a person has gone down into "the valley of the shadow of death" in suffering, his own heart is made more tender and he can better see the value of a kind word, a handclasp, and a comforting pat on the shoulder. With what tenderness and thanksgiving the sufferer remembers the person who said a kind word for or who has prayed for him.

Suffering helps one to see that the darkest hours may precede those which are brightest. Someone has well said that cowards die a thousand deaths before they really die. Men of deep faith and great courage die but once. Those of little faith and small courage often give up in despair when, without their realizing it, they were on the verge of victory. Many people in moments of utter despair have taken their own lives when, if they had but had the faith, patience, and courage to hold on a little longer, the darkness of despair would have vanished with the brightness of better things to come. The story is told of a man who, on an intensely cold, dark night during which a blizzard was blowing, trudged wearily almost all night through deep drifts of snow and against a driving, cutting north wind. Finally, after looking and looking for some kind of shelter, in despair and discouragement he sank to the snow-covered ground and went to sleep. The next morning a farmer opened his door and saw the man's outstretched fingers, now frozen in death, only a few feet from the door through which he would have found warmth, food, and continued life! He gave up a few seconds too soon. A person enduring suffering is much like a horseman riding through a dark forest in a deep, rocky valley with many dangers all about. While

going down into the valley, the horseman may despair
of ever getting out of it and back up on the mountain
where the sun is shining brightly. But without his even
being aware of it, the ground begins to rise gradually,
the trees to thin out, and the rocks to grow smaller. Then
suddenly he bursts out of the forest and on top of the
mountain and lo! — the sun is shining brightly! With
great joy, the rider turns in his saddle and surveys the
dark, rocky valley through which he has just ridden and
says to himself, "Why was I anxious while I was down
there? Why did I not trust my Lord? Besides, now that
I am here, I can see that the valley is not nearly so bad
as it looked to me while I was down there!"

May every sufferer learn well this lesson.

*Suffering helps the sufferer to realize that some moun-
tain heights can be reached only by going through the
valley which is in front of the mountain.* Paul taught
that some spiritual heights are reached by way of the
valley of affliction and tears.[17] After Manasseh went
down into a valley, he repented of his wickedness and
humbled himself before God.[18] Moses plainly taught the
Children of Israel that their afflictions would cause them
to return to the Lord.[19]

Affliction causes many to intensely desire to know the
word of God. Affliction even helps one to learn what

17. II Corinthians 4:17, 18.
18. II Chronicles 33:10-12.
19. Deuteronomy 4:40.

the will of God is. The Psalmist said, "It is good for me that I have been afflicted; that I might learn thy statutes."[20]

May every sufferer allow his suffering to tender his heart and cause him to walk closer to God.

Earthly fathers chasten their children because they love them. God also chastens those whom He loves. On this matter, the writer of the Epistle to the Hebrews said:

> And ye have forgotten the exhortation which speaketh unto you as unto children, My son, despise not thou the chastening of the Lord, nor faint when thou art rebuked of him: For whom the Lord loveth he chasteneth, and scourgeth every son whom he receiveth. If ye endure chastening, God dealeth with you as with sons; for what son is he whom the father chasteneth not? But if ye be without chastisement, whereof all are partakers, then are ye bastards, and not sons. Furthermore we have had fathers of our flesh which corrected us, and we gave them reverence: shall we not much rather be in subjection unto the Father of spirits, and live? For they verily for a few days chastened us after their own pleasure; but he for our profit, that we might be partakers of his holiness. Now no chastening for the present seemeth to be joyous, but grievous: nevertheless afterward it yieldeth the peaceable fruit of righteousness unto them which are exercised thereby. Wherefore lift up the hands which hang down, and the feeble knees; And make straight paths for your feet, lest that which is lame be turned out of the way; but let it rather be healed.[21]

When the Lord sees that a person needs a "thorn in the

---

20. Psalms 119:71.
21. Hebrews 12:5-13.

flesh" (some form of suffering), He gives it to him. When he sees that the "thorn" is needed as an *abiding* condition (a continuing source of suffering), then He allows that "thorn" to continue.[22] God did not remove Paul's "thorn in the flesh" even though Paul earnestly besought Him to do so. God knew better than Paul knew what Paul needed.

Those who suffer must have confidence in the Lord to give what is needed most. Just as human fathers at times must make decisions and do things which their children cannot understand, just so God's thoughts are above man's thoughts.[23] In denying Paul's request to have the "thorn in the flesh" removed, the Lord said to Paul, "My grace is sufficient for thee: for my strength is made perfect in weakness."[24]

In order to prepare certain men to perform a particular mission, by His providence, God brings men into situations of suffering.

It is evident that Paul *needed* a "thorn in the flesh" to prevent his becoming puffed up with pride. Because he had the "thorn," Paul reached and maintained spiritual heights which he would not have reached without it.

This is a fact which every sufferer should carefully note and treasure in his heart.

---

22. II Corinthians 12:7-10.
23. Isaiah 55:8, 9.
24. II Corinthians 12:9.

Suffering shows the sufferer the value of tears. Suffering may tender the soul and make the sufferer more keenly aware of the suffering of others. It may help the sufferer to "weep with them that weep."[25]

Suffering may cause a sinner to repent and turn to God. There are two marvelous passages in the 119th Psalm which plainly teach that suffering may cause a sinner to repent of his wickedness and turn to God with a truly penitent heart in readiness to live as God would have him to live.

In one of these passages, the Psalmist says, "Before I was afflicted I went astray, but now have I kept thy word."[26]

The other passage says, "It is good for me that I have been afflicted that I might learn thy statutes."[27]

The Psalmist recognized the value of his affliction in bringing him back to pathways of righteousness.

Reference has already been made to the story of Manasseh, king of Judah. At one time during his reign, Manasseh was a very wicked king. Of him, the inspired writer said, "So Manasseh made Judah . . . to err, and to do worse than the heathen . . ."[28] Further, of Manasseh it is said, "And the Lord spake to Manasseh, and to his peo-

---

25. Romans 12:15.
26. Psalms 119:67.
27. Psalms 119:71.
28. II Chronicles 33:9.

ple: but they would not hearken."[29] When all seemed to be going well with Manasseh and his subjects, his life was wicked, and his heart was hard. He would not listen to the Lord and turn from his sin. But the Lord went into action and brought affliction upon Manasseh.

> Wherefore the Lord brought upon them the captains of the host of the king of Assyria, which took Manasseh among the thorns, and bound him with fetters, and carried him to Babylon.[30]

That affliction caused Manasseh to humble himself before God. "And when he was in affliction, he besought the Lord his God, and humbled himself greatly before the God of his fathers, and prayed unto him: . . ."[31] The Lord heard his prayer and "brought him again to Jerusalem into his kingdom."[32] The happy result of Manasseh's affliction was, "Then Manasseh knew that the Lord he was God."[33]

During one of his addresses to the people of Israel, Moses warned them that if they fell away from serving the one true living God and turned aside to serve idols, then the Lord would bring great tribulation upon them. But, Moses promised, if in the midst of their tribulation they would repent of their sin and turn to God, He would forgive them.

---

29. II Chronicles 33:10.
30. II Chronicles 33:11.
31. II Chronicles 33:12, 13.
32. II Chronicles 33:13.
33. Ibid.

The same basic promise is given to people living today. Each sufferer should allow his suffering to cause him to walk closer to God. Even those who have been living good lives can strive to live even better. Suffering can be a great aid in reaching that goal.

Many people are now children of God because of some suffering or affliction which came into their lives. One person may have been led to turn to God because his body was afflicted with a terrible disease. Another person may have turned to God because of the loss of a dearly beloved wife or child. Another may have been led to turn to God because all of his worldly wealth was lost.

"Before I was afflicted I went astray, but now have I kept thy word."[34]

Suffering may help the sufferer to better understand that faith comes by hearing. Suffering may drive the sufferer to study God's word with more sincerity and with a more profound purpose. Those who properly react to suffering are driven to learn — and to weave into their hearts — the sublime truths concerning the providence, the goodness, the wisdom, and mercy and the love of God.[35] Such truths cannot be learned from the books of mere men. They must be learned from God's book, the Bible,[36] and by people whose hearts are tender, receptive, and eagerly seeking to know God's will for man.

---

34. Psalms 119:67.
35. Psalms 139; I Corinthians 1:18ff.
36. II Timothy 3:16, 17; II Peter 1:20, 21.

"So then faith cometh by hearing, and hearing by the word of God."[37]

At times, according to mere human knowledge and wisdom, the sufferer will cry, "This suffering is not good for me; God is not good to allow it to continue." But men must remember that God chastens those whom He loves.[38] (Of course, as previously explained, not all suffering is God's chastening.) As previously explained, when God sees that a person needs a "thorn in the flesh," such as Paul had, He gives it to him. When He sees that the "thorn" is needed as an *abiding* thing in one's life, He allows it to remain. God's children must trust in God to give what they most need. At times human fathers must do for their children what the children cannot understand to be best for them. In spite of the lack of understanding by the children, the parents must go ahead with what they know is best. In the same way, even though His children do not always understand, God goes ahead with what is best for them. At times, it is best for them that they endure suffering.

Suffering helps the sufferer to see the value of meditation. Many people feel that they are much too busy to ever stop and meditate upon spiritual matters. Many people do not so meditate until extreme suffering drives them to it. Then they can see its value and will find the time for a true self-examination. As did the Psalmist, all

37. Romans 10:17.
38. Hebrews 12,

men need to cry for divine aid in knowing their own
hearts, "Search me, O God, and know my heart: try me,
and know my thoughts: and see if there be any wicked
way in me, and lead me in the way everlasting."[39]

*Suffering helps the sufferer to see that there are human
hearts in which the milk of human kindness dwells.* Because they have encountered so much evil in the world,
many people grow cynical. They come to believe that
few, if any, people truly love goodness and righteousness
and practice kindness. It is profoundly enriching, when
in the midst of suffering, for one to learn that many
people love and serve their fellowmen because of their
deep love for God. Then the sufferer comes to understand more of "the tie that binds our hearts in Christian
love."

*Suffering helps the sufferer to see how easy it was
for him to bear the suffering of others.* When a person
truly suffers, he comes to understand that it is very difficult (if indeed, not impossible) for others to understand the various aspects of that suffering. Jesus sees the
suffering as it is to the sufferer, but mere men cannot
thus see it. Jesus also perfectly sees suffering as it should
be seen by the sufferer. But, again, mere man cannot thus
see it. The one who suffers can remember occasions in
his own life when, while visiting a person who was suffering, he somewhat casually and lightly (without any

---

39. Psalms 139:23, 24.

real conception of what the sufferer was undergoing) urged the sufferer to "keep your chin up" or stated some other worthless platitude. Those who have never truly suffered can usually bear better the malignancy of another person than a pin-scratch on their own hand. But suffering allows one to learn something of the burden which others must endure and to truly sympathize with that burden.

Suffering gives the sufferer an opportunity to "begin anew." Suffering may lead to the kind of personal soul-searching which causes one to ask himself, "What kind of person am I? Where am I right now? In what direction am I headed? What are my real goals in life? What is my relationship with God? Am I a hypocrite? What are the real motives in my heart? What am I in the dark?

To ask oneself these questions honestly is usually to bring forth answers which show that a number of changes should be made in one's life. This usually leads to efforts to make a new life.

In a sense, then, suffering can be said to provide the sufferer with an opportunity to "begin anew" to build the kind of life God would have him to build.

Instead of reacting in bitterness against God, each sufferer should recognize that because of his suffering, he and his family may be richly blessed.

CHAPTER VI

THE DANGERS OF SUFFERING

As discussed in the preceding chapter, suffering can be of great benefit in many different ways. However, for suffering to benefit the sufferer, he must react to that suffering in the way God would have him to react.

When one does not properly react to it, instead of being beneficial, suffering can be very destructive.

Suffering can cause one to despair. While he is marching in review on the parade ground, the soldier does not really know if he is a man of courage or not. The parade ground is not the place where courage is manifested. Being sharply dressed and marching in a straight line does not necessarily prove that a soldier will be brave and stand his ground when the first mortar shell bursts near enough for fragments to whine as they pass his head.

A soldier may be able to recite all of the military laws and regulations, he may sharply salute all of his officers every day, he may clean his rifle until it shines and then still prove to be a coward during his first moments of battle. When the going gets rough, he may desert his comrades, flee for his life and endanger the lives of the others as a result of his own cowardice.

At times, the men who bragged the most on the parade

ground back home were the most cowardly in the actual battle. Some times a man's true colors are not shown until the battle begins.

This same principle applies to spiritual matters. Some people may make strong affirmations of faith in the Lord — that is, until life strikes them a hard blow. While the sun is shining, some people loudly profess confidence in the goodness and providence of God as the Father of His children, but when the storm strikes they are soon whimpering about the cruelty of life and are murmuring against God as being devoid of mercy and compassion.

As has already been discussed, at times Satan "obtains" men to cast them into the fire of tribulation. Satan does this to destroy faith and damn the soul. God chastens in order to lead the person to repentance and resulting obedience. Satan acts out of hatred with the desire to destroy.[1] God acts out of love with the desire to save.[2]

Just as some soldiers despair in the heart of military battle, so some professed followers of Christ despair under the burden of suffering. Some simply lack the courage and faith required to endure. Some endure well for a while but they cannot stand under a burden that does not end as soon as they feel it should.

Some, not understanding Bible teaching regarding the will and purposes of God (previously discussed in this

1. I Peter 5:8.
2. John 3:16; Romans 5:8, 9.

book) fall into despair because they come to believe that God no longer loves them. They reason in this fashion: (1) if God loved me, He would not allow me to suffer over a long period of time; (2) yet God has allowed me to suffer for a long time — and is still allowing me to suffer; (3) therefore, I know God does not love me.

But it is not true that if God allows one to suffer such suffering is proof that God does not love the sufferer. God did not remove Paul's "thorn in the flesh" even though Paul earnestly besought Him to do so. Paul needed that "thorn," and it was because of love that God allowed the "thorn" to continue to prick him.

May no sufferer fall into the pit of despair because of suffering. May every sufferer know that God is man's refuge and fortress.[3] He is a sun and shield for those in trouble.[4] Let every sufferer turn to Him in faith. He will not turn His ear away from those who earnestly and honestly seek Him.[5]

Suffering may cause one to lose his faith in God. Some people who profess faith in the Lord Jesus Christ as the Son of God have never really studied the Bible. Because of this lack of study, they do not understand the will of God. They do not understand the relationship of sin, suffering, and the will of God. This matter was discussed in some detail in Chapter II, and, if the reader

---

3. Psalms 91:2.
4. Psalms 84:11, 12.
5. I Peter 3:10-12; Matthew 7:7-11.

feels the need, he is urged to re-read that chapter at this time.

Concerning the sin and suffering in the world, some people reason as follows: the existence of sin and suffering in the world proves that God is either: (1) *good* (and so wants to relieve man of his suffering) but *weak* (and so is unable to do what He wants to — that is, relieve man of his suffering), or (2) *evil* (and so wants man to continue in his suffering) and strong (and so is able to relieve man of his suffering if He wished to do so). But such reasoning is entirely false. God is both infinitely good and infinitely powerful. He wishes man to be only happy forever and forever. But in creating man, God gave to man the power to make choices for either righteousness or evil. Because man made wrong choices sin came into the world and suffering and death came as a result of sin. The reader should view suffering as it is discussed in the entirety of Bible teaching on the subject. God is all-wise, all-powerful, and everywhere present. God is love.[6] The fact that one (or one's loved ones) suffers is no ground for concluding that one should lose faith in God.

Rather, the time of suffering should be a time of most complete turning to God for the love, comfort, help and assurance which God wishes to give and will give.

The dangers of suffering may be overcome by (1)

---

6. I John 4:8,

properly preparing for suffering before it ever comes, and (2) by properly meeting it when it does come.

The following two chapters have much to do with the general subject of the present chapter. They should be read in the light of this fact.

CHAPTER VII

HOW TO PREPARE FOR SUFFERING

The need for preparing. The leaders of the United States are fully aware of the fact that this nation at any time may suffer an attack by a nation using nuclear weapons. Such a prospect is horrible even to contemplate. Yet, neither the leaders nor the people of this great nation have allowed the possibility of nuclear attack to cast them into the depths of despair. Rather, they are constantly seeking for better ways to prepare to meet and repel such an attack if it should come. No wise people will do less than this.

Both experience and the Bible teach that in much the same way any person may be cast at any time into a situation of extreme affliction and suffering. No one knows when such suffering might come to himself or to his loved ones — or both.

The work of Satan in connection with the affliction and trials of both Job and Peter[1] (as well as the rest of the Apostles) should be a warning to every person that suffering might come into the life of any one of us at any time. No one has any way of knowing if or when it will happen. Each person can only try to prepare for it as best he can.

1. Job 1, 2; Luke 22:31-34.

What can one do to prepare for suffering? Following are some suggestions as to some things which may be helpful.

One must come to understand that suffering sometimes comes to the righteous as well as to the wicked. Understanding this truth will guard one against the despair that causes one to cry, in rebellion against God, "Why am I suffering?" The various sources of causes of suffering must be understood.

One must build within his heart the attitude manifested by Job when he said, "though he slay me yet will I trust him."[2] Before suffering comes, each person should strive to realize that when suffering does come he may be bewildered by it. No one will have a direct explanation from God as to all of the ramifications of his own individual case. One must strive to prepare his heart to trust God in spite of whatever suffering and tribulation may come.

One must learn to view suffering from the standpoint of the benefits which can come as results of the suffering. Even suffering which comes as a result of one's own sin can be used to better one's life — provided he reacts to it as he should. One must not become bitter but must seek to profit from the suffering. One must seek to realize that when suffering comes, it may be that the Lord is bringing some needed chastening into one's life. One

2. Job 13:15.

should seek to realize that when suffering comes, it may be that the Lord is putting one into the crucible of affliction before making greater use of him. God does not take men down into the depths in order to overwhelm or destroy them. Suffering and affliction bring men back to God.[3]

One must come to understand that God knows each person individually. How easy it is for the sufferer to conclude, "No one loves me." This may very well be true so far as one's fellowmen are concerned, but it will not be true so far as *God* is concerned. God will never leave nor forsake His faithful children.[4] God knows every person by name. The very hairs of one's head are numbered by the Lord.[5] He, therefore, is acquainted with all of the problems of each and every person. He knows how those problems look to those who face them. In a sense, He can put Himself inside the mind of a person who is suffering and view that problem as it looks to the sufferer himself. How encouraging it can be to the sufferer to know that there is at least One who knows and understands what one feels in the depths of affliction and sorrow.[6]

One must come to understand that Satan knows men individually. According to the Bible, Satan knew Job, Peter, and the rest of the Apostles. He asked permission

3. Hosea 2:6, 7; Psalms 119:67, 71.
4. Hebrews 13:5.
5. Matthew 10:30.
6. Hebrews 2:18; 4:15,

to afflict Job and to sift the Apostles as wheat. He knows and wants to destroy (damn) each person. He seeks to bring upon men such conditions as will destroy their faith in God and in His word, the Bible. No one should underestimate the power of Satan, man's greatest adversary. Rather, each person should strive to so prepare himself as to be ready for whatever "sifting" Satan may bring about.

One must come to understand that the Lord requires that men be faithful in enduring these tests. In spite of the fact that Job's affliction was very severe, he had to endure in order to be pleasing to God. In spite of the facts that the trial of Peter was very severe, he had to repent and return to the Lord.[7]

One must come to understand that Christ prays for men that they may be strong in these tests. It is a source of great encouragement for a sufferer to know that someone is praying for him to be strong and of good courage. With such knowledge, the sufferer is much more likely to be strong. Christ also prays for men. He prayed for Peter that his faith fail not.[8] He will pray for men today that their faith fail not. The Holy Spirit helps the infirmities of man. Man does not know how to pray as he ought, but the Spirit makes intercession with groanings which cannot be uttered.[9]

---

7. John 21: I John 1:8-21.
8. Luke 22:31, 32.
9. Romans 8:26.

One should keep in mind that man lives on after this life is over. While he was in the midst of suffering, Job made it clear that he could accept and endure his suffering better if he could only know that he would live again after physical death. Paul explained this sublime truth in his second epistle to the church of Corinth.[10] He made it clear that even the most severe sufferings which men must endure in this life are not worthy to be compared with the blessings of eternal life in heaven with the Lord.[11] The hope of everlasting life[12] will serve as an anchor to the soul which may tend to drift away.[13]

One must recognize the place of prayer in God's plan for man. In spite of the fact that other children of God and even Christ Himself may pray for the sufferer, the one who suffers must also pray for himself. He must be sober and watch unto prayer.[14] He must gird up the loins of his mind in order to have the strength of character which is necessary to face and endure severe suffering in the right way.[15] Prayer plays a vital role in developing such character. Tribulation causes one to pray,[16] but one should not wait to pray until suffering comes. A devout prayer life should be a vital part of the *pre-*

---

10. II Corinthians 4:17, 18.
11. Romans 8:17, 18.
12. Titus 1:2.
13. Hebrews 6:19.
14. I Peter 4:7.
15. I Peter 1:13.
16. Psalms 79:8.

paration which one makes to meet whatever suffering may come.

One must seek to understand something of God's reaction to man's prayer. Men must learn that they must resign themselves to endure some situations. It is true that the Lord is infinite in wisdom, in power, in presence, in love, and in mercy. It is also true that He has taught men to ask for blessings with the promise that He will hear and answer their prayers.[17] But each person must also remember that even Jesus, the Son of God, when He prayed, said to the Father . . . "nevertheless not as I will, but as thou wilt."[18] Even so, men must pray for God's will, not their own will, to be done.

Also, men must learn that the time and way God answers prayer may vary according to needs of the individual doing the praying. At times, in answer to prayers, God may say (in effect), "Yes, I will give you this at once. That for which you have prayed is what you need at this very time." At other times, however, His answer may be, "Yes, I will give you that for which you have prayed, but you must have patience, for the time is not yet right for you to have it. I will give it to you later." At still other times, His answer may be, "No, I will not give you that for which you have prayed. You have asked for the wrong thing. Because I love you, I will not give you this for which you have asked, but

17. Matthew 7:7-11.
18. Matthew 26:39.

I will give you something else which you really do need."

Just so, at times men may pray for the release from suffering of either loved ones or themselves, but God's answer may be, "No, this is not what you need most."

It is appointed unto man once to die.[19] Death is the event which serves as the transition between this world and that which is to come. If the Lord answered every prayer for the sick with "Yes," then no one would ever die. So, men must resign themselves to this fact, for it is the will of God. Along with Job, one must sincerely say, "Though he slay me, yet will I trust him."

One must make his daily life a walk with Jesus, the Son of God. It is not likely that anything else is of greater importance in preparing for suffering. If one lives day by day trusting in material wealth and in other men rather than trusting in the Lord, it will be very hard indeed to transfer that trust to Christ when suffering comes. If one has been trusting in something or someone other than the Lord, when suffering comes and he sees those things upon which he has leaned swept away on a wave of worthlessness, then he is left with nothing upon which to lean for strength and he may plunge into despair.

One should make it a practice of his daily life to live just one day at a time. One must not try to carry the load of months or years which are yet to come. Rather,

19, Hebrews 9:27,

each person should strive to live as Jesus taught men to live: face and carry the burdens of only one day at a time.[20] If the sufferer begins to ask himself, "How long will I suffer?" the proper answer is, "Just *one* day at a time." If one makes this a habit of his life, when suffering does come, he will be able to more easily meet that burden only one day at a time.

One should make it a habit of his daily life to avoid anxiety. If the daily habit of one's life has been one of serenity and calmness rather than of anxiety and worry, then, when severe suffering comes, he will be better able to react to that suffering in harmony with Paul's instruction, "In nothing be anxious . . ."[21] Surely a proper preparation for suffering will include a careful and prayerful study of this passage. Among other valuable matters, the passage shows that men must not depend upon their own minds, or their own way of looking at things, to guard their hearts from fear and anxiety. Rather, through prayer and supplication, with *thanksgiving* (even in the midst of suffering) one should make his requests unto God. Then the peace of God, which passes all understanding, will guard him from fear and anxiety. Tribulation tests the sincerity and genuineness of one's faith.[22]

One should learn that in knowing us and loving us, Christ will not allow Satan to afflict or tempt him above

---

20. Matthew 6:34.
21. Philippians 4:6, 7, A.S.V.
22. Job 23:10.

or beyond that which he is able to bear. Some people come to believe that the trials and tribulations of life are too great to bear. But each person must remember that God placed some very definite limitations upon Satan's afflictions of Job. In the same vein, Paul taught ". . . God . . . will not suffer you to be tempted above that ye are able; but will with the temptation also make a way to escape, that ye may be able to bear it."[23] The Lord knows each person's individual weaknesses and the limitations of each person's ability to endure. He has promised that He will not allow Satan to tempt or try any one above that which they are able to bear. But each person must also remember that God, while providing a way of escape, is not going to *force* anyone to accept and travel that way. Each person must want it and accept it for himself. Fervent prayer is of tremendous aid in having the right desire and in making the right choice.

One must live a life of accepting Christ's invitation to "Come unto me all ye that labor and are heavy laden . . ."[24] This invitation is not an idle platitude, for it is an invitation from the Son of God. Those who truly believe in Him will regard this invitation with loving thanksgiving and with firm trust and confidence that the Lord *will* do just what He says He will do. In recognizing that suffering may come to any person, true believers will build their lives upon the firm rock that He will be

---

23. I Corinthians 10:13.
24. Matthew 11:28-30.

ready to receive them at any time they need Him to do so
— even when they are in the midst of severe suffering.
Thus, they will learn to be "patient in tribulation"[25] when
it does come.

As a further step in good preparation, *one must recognize the value of helping others in their tribulation.*
Of God, Paul said that He "comforteth us in all our
tribulation, that we may be able to comfort them which
are in any trouble, by the comfort wherewith we ourselves are comforted of God."[26] Thus it is seen that as one
receives comfort from God, he is, in turn, to comfort
others. As one comforts others he is made stronger to
endure his own suffering. This is true because spending
one's life in comforting others, he is walking in the
opposite direction from self-pity. He is thus turned in the
direction of thanksgiving for what blessings he does have
— in spite of what suffering may have to be endured.

*One must remember that an eternal home in heaven
— not a home in this world — is God's ultimate goal for
men.* Each person should live every day of his life with
this thought in mind. The attitude which will be thus
engendered will help one to overcome life's disappoint-
ments and to endure whatever suffering may come. This
life is the time of testing men's hearts and this world
is the *place* where the testing takes place. But this world
is not man's home. Each person must strive to have the

25. Romans 12:12.
26. II Corinthians 1:4.

attitude which Abraham had. Abraham and Sarah, his wife, confessed that they were strangers and pilgrims on the earth;[27] that is, they made it clear that they did not consider this world to be their home. They looked for the city "which hath foundations, whose builder and maker is God."[28] This same attitude was manifested by Paul when he said, "For me to live is Christ and to die is gain."[29] To believe whole-heartedly that heaven — not this world—is the eternal home of God's faithful children is of tremendous help to any person who is suffering severely.

---

27. Hebrews 11:13.
28. Hebrews 11:9.
29. Philippians 1:21,

CHAPTER VIII

HOW TO ENDURE SUFFERING
WITH PATIENCE

The writer of this book is keenly aware of how much easier it is to *tell* some sufferer how to patiently endure his suffering than it is to actually *show* him how to do it. Surely any mere human writer will feel inadequate in such matters so far as his own wisdom and character are concerned.

Yet, God has given His word, the Bible, to man, and it is to *that book* — not to the writer's wisdom or character — to which the reader is referred.

Much of what needs to be said as to what will help one to patiently endure suffering which has already come, has already been said in the preceding chapter on "How to Prepare for Suffering." Some of those points will be briefly repeated in this chapter; other points will not be repeated.

Following are some attitudes and practices which help the sufferer to patiently endure that suffering as God would have him to do it.

The sufferer should fill his mind with passages of comfort from the Bible. There *is* not—there *cannot* be—a substitute for a *daily, prayerful, devout* study of God's word. One should seek to study *all* of the Bible, yet during times of *severe* suffering, there are passages which are of special value. Here are some of them.

> The Lord is my shepherd; I shall not want.[1]
>
> Be careful for nothing; but in every thing by prayer and supplication with thanksgiving let your requests be made known unto God.
>
> And the peace of God, which passeth all understanding, shall keep your hearts and minds through Christ Jesus.[2]
>
> Humble yourselves therefore under the mighty hand of God, that he may exalt you in due time:
>
> Casting all your care upon him; for he careth for you.[3]
>
> The eternal God is *thy* refuge, and underneath *are* the everlasting arms: and he shall thrust out the enemy from before thee; and shall say, Destroy *them*.[4]
>
> The Lord also will be a refuge for the oppressed, a refuge in times of trouble.[5]
>
> For in the time of trouble he shall hide me in his pavilion: in the secret of his tabernacle shall he hide me; he shall set me up upon a rock. And now shall mine head be lifted up above mine enemies round about me: therefore will I offer in his tabernacle sacrifices of joy; I will sing, I will sing praises unto the Lord.[6]

---

1. Psalm 23:1.
2. Philippians 4:6, 7.
3. I Peter 5:6, 7.
4. Deuteronomy 33:27.
5. Psalm 9:9.
6. Psalms 27:5, 6.

I will be glad and rejoice in thy mercy: for thou hast considered my trouble; thou hast known my soul in adversities . . .[7]

I sought the Lord, and he heard me, and, and delivered me from all my fears.[8]

Many are the afflictions of the righteous: but the Lord delivereth him out of them all. He keepeth all his bones: not one of them is broken.[9]

God is our refuge and strength, a very present help in trouble.[10]

Cast thy burden upon the Lord, and he shall sustain thee: he shall never suffer the righteous to be moved.[11]

Thou tellest my wanderings: put thou my tears into thy bottle: are they not in thy book? When I cry unto thee, then shall mine enemies turn back: this I know: for God is for me.[12]

Truly my soul waiteth upon God: from him cometh my salvation. He only is my rock and my salvation; he is my defense; I shall not be greatly moved. How long will ye imagine mischief against a man? ye shall be slain all of you: as a bowing wall shall ye be, and as a tottering fence. They only consult to cast him down from his excellency: they delight in lies: they bless with their mouth, but they curse inwardly. Selah. My soul, wait thou only upon God; for my expectation is from him. He only is my rock and my salvation: he is my defence; I shall not be moved. In God is my salvation and my glory: the rock of my strength, and my refuge, is in God.[13]

7. Psalms 31:7.
8. Psalms 34:4.
9. Psalms 34:19, 20.
10. Psalms 46:1.
11. Psalms 55:22.
12. Psalms 56:8, 9.
13. Psalms 62:1-7.

My flesh and my heart faileth: but God is the strength of my heart, and my portion for ever.[14]

Unless the Lord had been my help, my soul had almost dwelt in silence.[15]

Like as a father pitieth his children, so the Lord pitieth them that fear him. For he knoweth our frame; he remembereth that we are dust.[16]

This is my comfort in my affliction: for thy word hath quickened me. The proud have had me greatly in derision: yet have I not declined from thy law. I remembered thy judgments of old, O Lord; and have comforted myself. Horror hath taken hold upon me because of the wicked that forsake thy law. Thy statutes have been my songs in the house of my pilgrimage.[17]

Unless thy law had been my delights, I should then have perished in mine affliction.[18]

In the day when I cried thou answeredst me, and strengthenedst me with strength in my soul.[19]

He healeth the broken in heart, and bindeth up their wounds.[20]

For thou hast been a strength to the poor, a strength to the needy in his distress, a refuge from the storm, a shadow from the heat, when the blast of the terrible ones is as a storm against the wall.[21]

For the people shall dwell in Zion at Jerusalem: thou shalt weep no more: he will be very gracious unto thee at the voice of thy cry; when he shall hear it, he will answer thee. And though the Lord give you the bread

14. Psalms 73:26.
15. Psalms 94:17.
16. Psalms 103:13, 14.
17. Psalms 119:50-54.
18. Psalms 119:92.
19. Psalms 138:3.
20. Psalms 147:3.
21. Isaiah 25:4,

of adversity, and the water of affliction, yet shall not thy teachers be removed into a corner any more, but thine eyes shall see thy teachers . . .[22]

Fear thou not; for I am with thee: be not dismayed; for I am thy God I will strengthen thee; yea, I will help thee; yea, I will uphold thee with the right hand of my righteousness.[23]

The Lord is good, a strong hold in the day of trouble; and he knoweth them that trust in him.[24]

Come unto me, all ye that labour and are heavy laden, and I will give you rest. Take my yoke upon you, and yearn of me; for I am meek and lowly in heart: and ye shall find rest unto your souls. For my yoke is easy, and my burden is light.[25]

Are not two sparrows sold for a farthing? and one of them shall not fall on the ground without your Father. But the very hairs of your head are all numbered. Fear ye not therefore, ye are of more value than many sparrows.[26]

These things I have spoken unto you that in me ye might have peace. In the world ye shall have tribulation: but be of good cheer; I have overcome the world.[27]

And we know that all things work together for good to them that love God, to them who are the called according to his purpose.[28]

Who shall separate us from the love of Christ? Shall tribulation, or distress, or persecution, of famine, or nakedness, or peril, or sword? As it is written, For thy sake we are killed all the day long; we are ac-

22. Isaiah 30:19, 20.
23. Isaiah 41:10.
24. Nahum 1:7.
25. Matthew 11:28-30.
26. Matthew 10:29-31.
27. John 16:33.
28. Romans 8:28.

counted as sheep for the slaughter. Nay, in all these things we are more than conquerors through him that loved us. For I am persuaded, that neither death, nor life, nor angels, nor principalities, nor powers nor things present, nor things to come. Nor height, nor depth, nor any other creature, shall be able to separate us from the love of God, which is in Christ Jesus our Lord.[29]

And he said unto me, My grace is sufficient for thee: for my strength is made perfect in weakness. Most gladly therefore will I rather glory in my infirmities, that the power of Christ may rest upon me.[30]

For in that he himself hath suffered being tempted, he is able to succour them that are tempted.[31]

For we have not an high priest which cannot be touched with the feeling of our infirmities; but was in all points tempted like as we are, yet without sin. Let us therefore come boldly unto the throne of grace, that we may obtain mercy, and find grace to help in time of need.[32]

Let your conversation be without covetousness; and be content with such things as ye have: for he hath said, I will never leave thee, nor forsake thee.[33]

Blessed is the man that endureth temptation: for when he is tried, he shall receive the crown of life, which the Lord hath promised to them that love him.[34]

There are many such comforting passages which assure the sufferer of the love of God. The sufferer is urged to

---

29. Romans 8:35-39.
30. II Corinthians 12:9.
31. Hebrews 2:18.
32. Hebrews 4:15, 16.
33. Hebrews 13:5.
34. James 1:12.

literally fill his heart with these and other such passages from God's sacred Word.

The sufferer should have a devout prayer life. The sufferer should pray many times every day. He should pray with deep and abiding faith that God will both hear and answer his prayer. That answer may not be just what the sufferer prayed for, but it will be that which was in harmony with God's will in the matter. As explained in a previous chapter, God's answer to prayer is: (1) sometimes, "No"; (2) sometimes, "wait"; (3) sometimes, "I will give you something else."

The attitude of the sufferer, as he prays, must be "not *my* will but *thine* be done." It must be that of Job when he said, "though he slay me yet will I trust him."

Following are some passages of Scriptures. These passages both urge men to pray and assure (under proper conditions) that the prayer will be both heard and answered.

> Seek the Lord and his strength, seek his face continually.[35]

> If my people, which are called by my name, shall humble themselves, and pray, and seek my face, and turn from. their wicked ways; then will I hear from heaven, and will forgive their sin, and will heal their land.[36]

---

35. I Chronicles 16:11.
36. II Chronicles 7:14.

The Lord is nigh unto all them that call upon him, to all that call upon him in truth.[37]

The sacrifice of the wicked is an abomination to the Lord: but the prayer of the upright is his delight.[38]

Seek ye the Lord while he may be found, call ye upon him while he is near.[39]

If thou afflict them in any wise, and they cry at all unto me, I will surely hear their cry.[40]

When thou art in tribulation, and all these things are come upon thee, even in the latter days, if thou turn to the Lord thy God, and shalt be obedient unto his voice; (For the Lord thy God is a merciful God:) he will not forsake thee, neither destroy thee, nor forget the covenant of thy fathers which he sware unto them.[41]

And thus, Solomon my son, know thou the God of thy father, and serve him a perfect heart and with a willing mind: for the Lord searcheth all hearts, and understandeth all the imaginations of the thoughts: if thou seek him, he will be found of thee; but if thou forsake him, he will cast thee off forever.[42]

And they that know thy name will put their trust in thee: for thou, Lord, hast not forsaken them that seek thee . . . When he maketh inquisition for blood, he remembereth them: he forgetteth not the cry of the humble.[43]

The eyes of the Lord are upon the righteous, and his ears are open unto their cry . . . The righteous cry,

37. Psalms 145:18.
38. Proverbs 15:8.
39. Isaiah 55:6.
40. Exodus 22:23.
41. Deuteronomy 4:30, 31.
42. I Chronicles 28:9.
43. Psalms 9:10, 12,

and the Lord heareth, and delivereth them out of all their troubles.[44]

Delight thyself also in the Lord; and he shall give thee the desires of thine heart. Commit thy way unto the Lord; trust also in him; and he shall bring it to pass.[45]

And call upon me in the day of trouble: I will deliver thee, and thou shalt glorify me.[46]

As for me, I will call upon God and the Lord shall save me. Evening, and morning, and at noon, will I pray, and cry aloud: and he shall hear my voice.[47]

For thou, Lord, art good, and ready to forgive; and plenteous in mercy unto all them that call upon thee. Give ear, O Lord, unto my prayer; and attend to the voice of my supplications. In the day of my trouble I will call upon thee: for thou wilt answer me.[48]

He shall call upon me, and I will answer him: I will be with him in trouble; I will deliver him, and honour him.[49]

He will regard the prayer of the destitute, and not despise their prayer. This shall be written for the generation to come: and the people which shall be created shall praise the Lord. For he hath looked down from the height of his sanctuary; from heaven did the Lord behold the earth; To hear the groaning of the prisoner; to loose those that are appointed to death.[50]

Let not mercy and truth forsake thee: bind them about thy neck; write them upon the table of thine heart: So shalt thou find favour and good understanding in

---

44. Psalms 34:15, 17.
45. Psalms 37:4, 5.
46. Psalms 50:15.
47. Psalms 55:16, 17.
48. Psalms 86:5-7.
49. Psalms 91:15.
50. Psalms 102:17-20.

the sight of God and man. Trust in the Lord with all thine heart; and lean not unto thine own understanding.[51]

The Lord is far from the wicked; but he heareth the prayer of the righteous.[52]

Then shall ye call upon me, and ye shall go and pray unto me, and I will hearken unto you. And ye shall seek me, and find me, when ye shall search for me with all your heart.[53]

Ask, and it shall be given you; seek, and ye shall find; knock, and it shall be opened unto you: For every one that asketh receiveth; and he that seeketh findeth; and to him that knocketh it shall be opened. Or what man is there, of you, whom if his son ask bread, will he give him a stone? Or if he ask a fish, will he give him a serpent? If ye then, being evil, know how to give good gifts unto your children, how much more shall your Father which is in heaven give good things to them that ask him?[54]

Again I say unto you, That if two of you shall agree on earth as touching anything that they shall ask, it shall be done for them of my Father which is in heaven. For where two or three are gathered together in my name, there am I in the midst of them.[55]

Let us therefore come boldly unto the throne of grace, that we may obtain mercy, and find grace to help in time of need.[56]

But without faith it is impossible to please him; for he that cometh to God must believe that he is and that he is a rewarder of them that diligently seek him.[57]

51. Proverbs 3:3-5.
52. Proverbs 15:29.
53. Jeremiah 29:12, 13.
54. Matthew 7:7-11.
55. Matthew 18:19, 20.
56. Hebrews 4:16.
57. Hebrews 11:6.

And this is the confidence that we have in him, that, if we ask any thing according to his will, he heareth us: And if we know that he hear us, whatsoever we ask, we know that we have the petitions that we desired of him.[58]

Be careful for nothing; but in everything by prayer and supplication with thanksgiving let your requests be made known unto God. And the peace of God, which passeth all understanding, shall keep your hearts and minds through Christ Jesus.[59]

Of all the above passages, even though each and every one contains great comfort and assurance, none have been of greater personal assurance and comfort to the writer of this book than Philippians 4:6, 7, I Peter 5: 7, Matthew 7:7-11, and Psalms 23. Perhaps other passages will be of greater comfort to others.

There are many other such passages in the Bible. The sufferer should search for and study them. Then every such passage possible should be treasured up in the heart of the sufferer. He then should earnestly pray *many* times every day. When one prays, he talks with God! When one studies God's word, the Bible, *God talks to him!*

The sufferer should carefully examine his heart and life with a view to honestly deciding if he is a faithful child of God. The Apostle Paul said, "Examine yourselves, whether ye be in the faith; prove your own selves."[60] To do this, the sufferer must both be honest

---

58. I John 5:14, 15.
59. Philippians 4:6, 7.
60. II Corinthians 13:5.

with himself and ask for God's help in conducting that self-examination.[61]

The sufferer should then repent of every sin of which he is aware. Repentance involves a change of mind.[62] It means the sinner has changed his mind regarding the sin in his life. It means that instead of loving sin (with the resulting intention to practice sin), the penitent person no longer either loves sin or intends to practice it. After repentance, one loves God and righteousness and hates sin.

After repenting of whatever sin may be in his life, the penitent person should whole heartedly do everything he knows (from the Bible) God would have him to do. Jesus said, "And why call ye me, Lord, Lord, and do not the things which I say?"[63] Christ is the author of eternal salvation to all them that obey him.[64] Those who do His will are the ones who enter the kingdom of God.[65] God will hear and answer the prayer of the obedient, but He will turn His face away from those who are living in rebellion to His will.[66]

What could be of more comfort to any sufferer than the firm assurance that he is living in harmony with the will of God? Because he had this assurance, Paul could

---

61. Psalms 139:23, 24.
62. Matthew 21:28-30.
63. Luke 6:46.
64. Hebrews 5:8, 9.
65. Matthew 7:21-23.
66. I Peter 3:12; John 9:31.

say, "For me to live is Christ . . ." Because he fought the good fight, kept the faith, and finished his course, Paul was assured that the crown of righteousness was laid up for him.[67]

It is when men draw nigh to God that God draws near to them.[68] Men must be willing to humble themselves in the sight of the Lord (live in harmony with His will) and then the Lord will lift them up.[69]

The sufferer must properly evaluate his suffering as over against the eternal weight of glory.[70] Of course, some suffering which is endured by some people in this life is truly intense from a human viewpoint. In spite of this fact, Paul said, "For our light affliction, which is but for a moment, worketh for us a far more exceeding and eternal weight of glory."[71] In comparison with the glories and blessings of heaven, suffering in this life is light — no matter how great that suffering may appear to man.

Every sufferer should treasure in his heart the sublime truth that this life with all of its affliction, adversity, suffering, sorrow, and tears will soon be over. Even the longest life on earth is but a moment in comparison with the unending ages of eternity.

---

67. II Timothy 4:6-8.
68. James 4:8.
69. James 4:10.
70. This matter was rather fully discussed in Chapter IV, so will not be discussed in much detail here.
71. II Corinthians 4:17.

The sufferer should live only one day at a time. In the discussion of what should be done to prepare for suffering, it was pointed out that one should make it a habit of his life to bear the burdens of only one day at a time. Jesus said, "Take no thought for the morrow: for the morrow shall take thought for the things of itself. Sufficient unto the day is the evil thereof."[72]

If a sufferer begins to be anxious about the burdens of many days, weeks, months, or years, he may well burden his spirit beyond the breaking point. The Lord Jesus has urged His children not to do this but to carry only the burdens of each day — one day at a time.

Through the Apostle Paul, Jesus taught that His children should not be anxious about anything.[73] Even though he who suffers will undergo at least short periods of depression, he must not allow himself to make these periods a pattern of his life.

One should turn his problems, his burdens, and cares over to the Lord and *trust* in Him to provide what is needed. To *trust* in the Lord means to truly have confidence in Him to do what He says He will do. The Lord will give strength to endure to His faithful children who ask Him.[74]

Let each sufferer remember that when he is "weakest"

---

72. Matthew 6:34.
73. Philippians 4:6, 7.
74. II Corinthians 12:7-9.

(that is, when he depends least on his own strength and most on the strength of the Lord), then he is, in fact, the "strongest."[75]

May each sufferer rid himself of worry and anxiety, and trust in the Lord for peace of mind comes to those who truly believe that they have adequate resources with which to meet the trial or suffering at hand.

On one occasion, Jesus and His disciples were in a ship. Jesus "was in the hinder part of the ship, asleep on a pillow."[76] A great storm of wind arose and the waves beat into the ship so that it was being filled with water. The disciples were afraid, and they awakened Jesus and said unto Him, "Master, carest thou not that we perish?"[77] Jesus calmly arose, rebuked the wind, and said unto the sea, "Peace, be still."[78]

Jesus then said to His disciples, "Why are ye so fearful? how is it that ye have no faith?"[79] He was asking, "How is it that you have no confidence in me?"

On this occasion, why was Jesus so calm in contrast to the fear of the disciples? Simply because He knew that He had adequate resources with which to meet the storm. Sufficient resources were also available to the disciples, but they did not have enough faith to lay hold upon those

---

75. II Corinthians 12:10.
76. Mark 4:38.
77. *Ibid.*
78. Mark 4:39.
79. Mark 4:40.

resources. Had they had such faith, they, too, could have had peace of mind even as did Jesus.

To every sufferer, who will humbly submit in faith and love to the will of God and obey His will as revealed in the Bible, resources which are adequate to meet every trial of life are available.

May every sufferer have sufficient faith (or confidence) in the Lord so that no matter how intense suffering may become, he may have peace of mind through the knowledge that he has at his disposal adequate resources from Christ with which to meet and bear that suffering.

The peace which Jesus gives is that which comes from having the resources to adequately meet the problem. The Lord will not allow His children to be tempted above that which they are able to bear.[80]

---

80. I Corinthians 10:13.

CHAPTER IX

SOME GOOD EXAMPLES OF HOW SUFFERING SHOULD BE ENDURED

The example of Job.[1] Job lost almost all upon which human hearts lean for support. He lost his wealth, his children, his health, his wife turned against him, to all intents and purposes he lost his friends. He also lost the sense of dignity of his own being. He lost his conviction that God ruled the universe — or, that if He did, He did not do it very well. Actually, he lost everything except his faith in God and a sense of himself as a creature of God. In spite of all this loss and suffering, Job could still say, "Though he slay me, yet will I trust him."[2]

All of this loss and suffering came to Job in spite of the fact that he was a good man. He was described as being perfect and upright. He feared God and hated evil. He was pure in both thought and conduct. He kept himself free from immorality. He was an honest man and was free of false pride.

He was thoughtful and courteous in his dealings with others. He was kind to his own family and to others. He was helpful to widows and orphans. He counseled with those in sorrow and sought to comfort and strengthen

---

1. The reader should read the entire book of *Job.*
2. Job 13:15.

them. He was free of inclination toward idolatry. He was a man of great stature in his community.

Yet, tragic and extreme suffering came upon such a good man. In facing this suffering Job did not sin. He did not, as many who suffer are prone to do, charge God foolishly.[3] He said that the Lord had given blessings and had now taken them away. He thus recognized the Lord's right to allow such to happen.

Satan[4] struck Job with extremely loathsome sores from head to foot. Job was then reduced to sitting in a rubbish heap, likely outside the walls of the town. He was then repulsive to himself and to others. His wife could have been a source of strength and comfort to him, but she also turned against him and counseled him to "curse God and die."[5] Apparently all but three of his friends had now forsaken him. These three came and sat in sympathy with Job for seven days before speaking. They then accused Job of sin and said that he was suffering because of his sin. Actually, they were a source of even more suffering rather than of comfort. Job called them "miserable comforters."[6]

As the three men continued to press their charges, out of the depth of his misery, Job cried: Why was I ever born? Being born, why did I not die at birth? Not dying

---

3. Job 1:22; 2:10.
4. Please read carefully Job 1:7-2:13.
5. Job 2:9.
6. Job 16:2. (This instance should be a good lesson to all who seek to comfort the suffering.)

at birth, why do I not now die? At this point, he had lost the sense of his own worth as an individual personality. Later, he also lost his grasp of the fact that God had been (and was) gracious to him. Still later, he seemed to have lost faith in the fact that God justly rules the world.

In fact, Job lost the things upon which human beings lean for strength. When one loses his possessions, he can usually gain strength and assurance from his children, his wife, his friends. If he still has his good health and his sense of his place and worth as an individual, he can gain strength and comfort from them and launch out anew. If one also loses (in addition to his wealth), his health and his children, he can still grasp the hand of his wife, and the two may give strength to one another. But when Job lost his wealth, his children, and his health, his wife also failed him. If, after his wife had failed him, he had retained his good health, he might have gone on alone. A healthy body gives one a vitality of outlook which is difficult to attain when one is in ill health. But even after Job had lost everything upon which many human beings depend, he retained his faith in the one true living God.[7]

In spite of suffering and loss which must have reached the very limit of what any human being could stand,[8]

---

7. This is true in spite of the fact that Job came to some wrong conclusions about God's dealings with man's suffering.
8. May every sufferer today measure his own suffering by that of Job.

Job made the basic reaction to his suffering which he should have made. He said, "Though he slay me, yet will I trust him."[9] It is not likely that there is a better statement of what man's reaction should be to suffering which he cannot understand. Many people have been bewildered and crushed by the suffering which came crashing into their lives. From this bewilderment, some have lost their faith in the goodness of God. Others have even lost their faith in the existence of God. But even if he could not understand, Job was determined to trust God anyway.

In His reply to Job's bewilderment, God pointed out to Job that there are many things about the physical world (which was created by God) which he (Job) did not understand. Since this was true, he should not expect to understand everything about God's dealings with man (also a creation of God).

Job humbled himself to accept this viewpoint. He thus became a wonderful example for every other sufferer to follow. May every sufferer continue to trust God even when he cannot understand his suffering.

The example of Joseph.[10] The suffering of Joseph did not come from physical illness. Rather, he was mistreated by his own brothers and unjustly punished by a government official.

---

9. Job 13:15.
10. The reader should study carefully Chapter 37 through Chapter 50 of the book of Genesis.

Because of jealousy,[11] the brothers of Joseph sold him into slavery to a company of Ishmaelites.[12] These men then took him to Egypt and sold him to a man named Potiphar, an officer of Pharaoh. The Lord was with Joseph and he was made overseer of Potiphar's house and was put in charge of all Potiphar's possessions. But day by day Potiphar's wife sought to seduce Joseph into immorality. He refused because he would not sin against God. After being thus rejected, Potiphar's wife bore false witness against Joseph and accused him of the very sin of which she herself was guilty. Because of this, Joseph was cast into prison.[13]

However, even while Joseph was in prison the Lord was with him and caused him to gain the favor of the keeper of the prison.

Even though none of his suffering was deserved, Joseph calmly and patiently retained his great faith in God. He thus affords every sufferer today a wonderful example of how to react to and endure punishment of suffering which is not deserved.

The example of Paul. The suffering and trials of Paul are well described in the following passages from the Scriptures.

For I think that God hath set forth us the apostles

11. Over the fact that Joseph was the favorite of their father, Genesis 37:4.
12. Genesis 37:23-28.
13. Genesis 39:6-20.

last, as it were appointed to death: for we are made a spectacle unto the world, and to angels, and to men.[14]

For we would not, brethren have you ignorant of our trouble which came to us in Asia, that we were pressed out of measure, above strength, in so much that we despaired even of life: But we had the sentence of death in ourselves, that we should not trust in ourselves, but in God which raiseth the dead.[15]

We are troubled on every side, yet not distressed; we are perplexed, but not in despair; Persecuted, but not forsaken; cast down, but not destroyed; Always bearing about in the body the dying of the Lord Jesus, that the life also of Jesus might be made manifest in our body. For we which live are always delivered unto death for Jesus' sake, that the life also of Jesus might be made manifest in our mortal flesh.[16]

But in all things approving ourselves as the ministers of God, in much patience, in afflictions, in necessities, in distresses, in stripes, in imprisonments, in tumults, in labours, in watchings, in fastings; By pureness, by knowledge, by long sufferings, by kindness, by the Holy Ghost, by love unfeigned, by the word of truth, by the power of God, by the armour of righteousness on the right hand and on the left. By honour and dishonour, by evil report and good report: as deceivers, and yet true: As unknown, and yet well known: as dying, and behold, we live; as chastened, and not killed; As sorrowful, yet always rejoicing; as poor, yet making many rich; as having nothing, and yet possessing all things.[17]

In spite of this extreme adversity, Paul had such faith in the Lord and such a sublime hope of everlasting

---

14. I Corinthians 4:9.
15. II Corinthians 1:8, 9.
16. II Corinthians 4:8-11.
17. II Corinthians 6:4-10.

100 A SUN AND SHIELD

life that he could say, ". . . for I am ready not to be bound only, but also to die at Jerusalem for the name of the Lord Jesus."[18]

Even from a prison cell, Paul wrote to the Philippians, "Rejoice in the Lord alway; and again I say, Rejoice."[19]

To the same people, he said, "For me, to live is Christ . . ."[20] and "In nothing be anxious . . ."[21]

Paul had this attitude because he knew he was a son of God[22] and had lived a faithful life in harmony with Christ's will.[23]

> As it is written, For thy sake we are killed all the day long; we are accounted as sheep for the slaughter. Nay, in all these things we are more than conquerors through him that loved us.[24]

Every sufferer should strive to develop the attitudes which Paul had and to patiently face adversity as he did. When Paul had to endure a "thorn in the flesh," he endured it patiently as being God's will and as being for his own good.[25]

The example of Jesus Christ, or Lord. The Lord knew that the suffering of the cross was coming to Him, and He faced it with resolution. He steadfastly set His face

18. Acts 21:13.
19. Philippians 4:4.
20. Philippians 1:21.
21. Philippians 4:6.
22. Galatians 3:26. 27; Romans 6:3-5.
23. II Timothy 4:6-8.
24. Romans 8:35-37.
25. II Corinthians 12:7-10,

toward that suffering[26] — nothing could deter Him from doing the will of the Father.

His life was characterized by prayer long before the crucifixion occurred. He also prayed[27] while in the very shadow of the cross. He prayed that the "cup"[28] might pass from Him. Nevertheless, He conditioned that request with the modification, ". . . nevertheless, not as I will, but as thou wilt."[29]

It was during prayer that He won the battle over suffering. He arose from this prayer and met, with utter calmness and serenity, those who were to crucify Him.

He met suffering without self-pity. In fact, even on the way to Golgotha,[30] He showed concern for others rather than for Himself.[31]

He chose suffering over sin, and today He commands all men to make that same choice: choose suffering over sin.[32]

The prayer of Christ in Gethsemane was heard but not for deliverance from the suffering. Rather, He received the strength to bear the suffering.[33]

---

26. The crucifixion and all accompanying events.
27. In the Garden of Gethsemane, Matthew 26.
28. That is, of suffering.
29. Matthew 26:39.
30. Where Jesus was crucified.
31. Luke 23:27-31.
32. Revelation 2:10; cf.: II Corinthians 12:7-10.
33. Hebrews 5:7-10; cf.; II Corinthians 12:7-10.

Every sufferer should treasure these sublime truths in His truth. Christ left men an example so that in meeting suffering they might walk in His steps.

> For even hereunto were ye called: because Christ also suffered for us, leaving us an example, that ye should follow his steps: Who did no sin, neither was guile found in his mouth: Who, when he was reviled, reviled not again; when he suffered, he threatened not; but committed himself to him that judgeth righteously.[34]

---

34. I Peter 2:21-23.

CHAPTER X

SOME LESSONS LEARNED AND
SOME CONCLUSIONS DRAWN

From the matters noted and discussed previously in this book, there are some very valuable lessons which should be learned and some very definite conclusions which should be drawn.

It is possible to continue in faith even after all human "props" have been swept away. In the book of *Job*, there is the record of Satan's contending that no man serves God for nought. He maintained that no man would serve God simply because of his love for God. But Job continued to have faith in God in spite of the loss of all things upon which human beings usually lean for strength. The Apostle Paul was a New Testament example of a man's having that sort of faith. Paul counted all things as loss for Christ.[1]

Hypocrites make a *pretense* of serving God so that they may receive the praises of men,[2] but adversity such as that endured by Job will ordinarily make manifest all such hypocrisy.

If Job and Paul could continue to faithfully serve

---

1. Philippians 3:7, 8.
2. Matthew 6:1-4.

God in spite of the trials they faced, then those who suffer adversity today can also remain faithful.

The proper reaction to suffering is to trust in God even when bewildered by the suffering. In His speech to Job, God explained neither about His meeting with Satan nor about the accusations and request made by Satan. He did not explain about the test for which he had given permission to Satan. No doubt, if Job had known all of these details, it would have been much easier for him to have borne all of the suffering. But God did not explain. He did not explain about the request of Satan. He did not explain the details about the Coming Redeemer.[3] He gave no explanation of the general problem of suffering.

Why was God silent on all of these problems which plagued the soul of this good man? Because it was His desire that Job would continue to trust Him in spite of not having the answers to these problems.

Instead of giving Job the answers to the questions which were on his mind, God asked Job a series of questions. These questions led Job to face the fact that he did not understand all about God's physical creation. From this fact, he was led to the conclusion that he could not expect to understand all about God's dealings with another of His creations: man. Job had to trust God

---

3. At least, at this given point He did not.

even when he could not understand all of the ramifications of his suffering.

In the same way, those who suffer today must trust God even when they cannot understand all of the various aspects of their own individual cases. Of course men living today have much explanation of God's dealings with man which Job did not have, but, even so, no one will be able to understand all about every case of suffering.

Righteous men, as well as evil ones, may suffer during this life. Over and over Job's friends contended that he was suffering because of sin in his life. But their contention was not true. Job suffered in spite of the fact that he was a righteous man.

Jesus also plainly refuted the theory that only evil men suffer. He said that the Galileans whose blood by Pilot was mingled with their own sacrifices were not sinners above all other Galileans. Nor, He said, were the eighteen upon whom the tower of Siloam fell the greatest offenders among the men of Jerusalem.[4] If the theory advanced by Job's friends were true, then those who suffer the most would be the greatest sinners. Jesus denied this theory. He also pointed out that the blindness of the man born blind was not the result of sins committed either by the man himself or by his parents.[5]

---

4. Luke 13:1-5.
5. John 9:1-3.

Man's suffering *may* be the result of his own sins, for Paul plainly taught that men reap what they sow.[6]

With God's help,[7] the sufferer should search his soul and strive earnestly to recognize any wicked way within himself, but he should not punish himself unnecessarily by believing that *all* suffering is the result of one's own sins.

Exact justice is not always gained in this life. At times, the righteous suffer from both pain and poverty while the wicked prosper in both health and wealth. This situation strikes a death blow to the faith of some. But God's children must remember that this life is not all there is to man. When man dies, he *will* live again! Christ will raise all from the dead.[8] The Judgment, at which all will be present, will follow.[9] Then the wicked will be cast into everlasting punishment, but the righteous will go away into everlasting life.[10]

No one can properly evaluate suffering who does not understand these facts.

But suffering may be God's chastening of those He loves. The Bible plainly teaches that God chastens His children.[11] He does this to help them recognize the sin in their lives, to cause them to turn away from that sin,

---

6. Galatians 6:7-9.
7. Psalms 139:23, 24.
8. John 5:28, 29.
9. Matthew 25:30, 31; Hebrews 9:27.
10. Matthew 25:46.
11. Hebrews 12:6.

and to help them remain humble. Let no sufferer despise the chastening of God. God chastens His children that they "might be partakers of his holiness."[12] May each person who suffers remember that "no chastening for the present seemeth to be joyous, but grievous; nevertheless afterward it yieldeth the peacable fruit of righteousness unto them which are exercised thereby."[13]

There are some dangers connected with suffering. Because they fail to understand the message of the book of *Job* and other portions of the Scriptures, some sufferers fall into extreme spiritual despondency, lose their faith and fall away from God. Job came close to this, but he retained his faith in God.

In spite of their understanding of this teaching some simply are unable to reconcile themselves to the suffering which either they themselves or one of their loved ones must endure. Such people usually become unfaithful to God.

Reaction to suffering of whatever nature the suffering may be, is quite a crucial thing in the life of any person. Those who suffer must trust in God as their loving Father. They must be faithful even unto (the point of) death in order to receive the crown of life.[14]

Those who suffer must recognize and lay hold on those

12. Hebrews 12:10.
13. Hebrews 12:11.
14. Revelation 2:10.

things which help one to properly react to suffering. Suffering will either help or harm those who suffer. Whether one is helped or harmed will depend upon the reaction which he makes to it. There are some things which are vital to a proper reaction. One of these things is the realization that the relatively short period of time during which people suffer in this life is not worthy to be compared with the glory and the blessings which await those who spend eternity with the Lord in heaven.[15]

Suffering cannot be understood apart from understanding the "will of God." God created man in His own image and gave him the capacity to make, among other things, spiritual and moral choices. He gave to man the intellectual and spiritual capacities which made it possible for him to either love or hate God Himself. In so doing, God made it possible for man to either obey or disobey His commandments.[16] In creating man, it was God's will that man would always be happy, that he would always be free from suffering or sorrow of any kind. And man would have always been such *if* he had continued to be obedient to God's will. But man sinned,[17] and, in sinning, by his own choice, he brought upon himself the results of sin: loss of fellowship with God,[18]

---

15. Romans 8:18.
16. Genesis 3:1-7.
17. Genesis 1:27; 2:15-17.
18. Isaiah 59:1, 2.

pain, suffering, death, and so on. Paul said, "The wages of sin is death."[19]

The fact that there is suffering in the world does not mean that God wished this to be the case. It was God's ideal will that man would never sin and so would never suffer and never die. But in order for man to have the capacity to love God (and so *serve* Him by *choice*), God had to give man the capacity *not* to love Him (and to disobey Him by *choice*). When man made the wrong choice, he brought suffering into the world.[20]

All should seek to prepare for whatever suffering may come. No one can be sure that he will escape suffering. Each person should recognize that he may soon be plunged into the depths of grief and suffering. Yet this fact should not cause people to live in *fear* of suffering but should cause them to do their very best to make proper preparation to meet it if it should come.[21] Godly living and a devout prayer life are vital to such preparation.

Christ has a vital part in proper reaction to suffering. Those who suffer need someone who understands their suffering and who, at the same time, can be their Advocate with God. Jesus Christ, the Son of God, meets this need.[22] Suffering man knows he is unworthy to approach the

---

19. Romans 6:23.
20. A more detailed discussion of this entire point is found in Chapter II.
21. A more detailed discussion of this point is found in Chapter VII.
22. Hebrews 2:18; I John 2:1.

throne of God, but he sees his *need* to do so. This was the reason Job cried out for a "daysman," someone who could put his hand on both man and God.

Christ has "been tempted in all points like as we," not in the sense that He has actually endured each and every possible item of human suffering or temptation but in the sense that in enduring the greatest suffering of all (the indescribable agony of the cross), He is involved in every lesser suffering which man might have to endure.[23] Because He suffered, being tempted, He is able to help those who are tempted because of their suffering. He understands and sees the suffering as it actually looks to the one who is suffering. With this feeling and understanding, He is the mediator between man and God. He died for man's sins, He arose from the dead,[24] and is now seated on His throne as King over His kingdom.[25] He, "ever liveth to make intercession."[26] for man.

"Be of good cheer" (of good *courage*) our Lord has overcome the world.[27]

What a friend we have in Jesus — to help us bear all of our sorrows and trials.

---

23. Hebrews 4:15.
24. I Corinthians 15:1-4.
25. Acts 2:30-36.
26. Hebrews 7:25.
27. John 16:33.